Inventions = Money

Dirk D. Brown, PH.D.

Dale C. Hogue, Sr. ESQ.

Published by Grey Gold Advisors, LLC

ISBN 978-0-9962493-0-0 (paperback).

Also published in eBook format.

Printed in the United States of America.

To our families

with deepest gratitude

for their unconditional support

Contents

Preface

Intellectual property in the form of patents and trade secrets can provide compelling value for an individual or enterprise. In almost all companies today, intellectual property plays an increasingly important role in competitive positioning and represents a growing fraction of the overall enterprise value.

The material in this book focuses on how to document and process inventions into assets that may later become intellectual property in the form of either a patent or a trade secret.

Harvesting the work of innovators is the first and essential step in creating valuable patents. *Human knowledge* must be recorded for it to become an *intellectual asset*. After it is an asset it may be further made into *intellectual property* by complying with the laws of the country in which it resides. One outcome is to apply for and receive a patent. Another is to keep the invention a trade secret.

This text and the accompanying exercises will help prepare you to function as a patent engineer (scientist) in an innovation enterprise. It teaches skills to identify, record, and manage the process of creating intellectual property. It also addresses the development of patents that accurately capture the subject invention and most effectively further the objectives of the enterprise.

This text focuses on developing inventions into patents and trade secrets to create value for an enterprise. Other forms of intellectual property, such as trademarks and copyrights derived from creative works, can also provide compelling value for an individual or enterprise but are not addressed here.

This text is based upon United States of America patent law and practice. It may be applicable to countries with similar legal systems. The materials are organized to build a knowledge base to be used in following sections. It is recommended that the readings and exercises be followed sequentially and not taken out of order to get the most from the learning experience.

Writing clearly and accurately is a prerequisite to being an effective patent engineer. If this is a challenge for you, it is recommended that you first get help in this area through coursework or independent study. You should also be able to decipher technical material and have the tenacity to follow up with inventors to complete an accurate description of inventions. You may also be called upon to conduct prior art searches or at least review them to help in better describing inventions (patent-eligible inventions cannot include prior art) and managing the patent application process.

Welcome to the innovation profession.

Dirk D. Brown, PhD,
Director of Faber Entrepreneurship Center
Moore School of Business, University of South Carolina
Dirk.Brown@Moore.sc.edu

Dale C. Hogue, Sr.
Patent Attorney
Grey-Gold Advisors, LLC
Dale@Grey-Gold.com

Introduction

The first step in the patent process is to document the invention. *Intellectual capital*, such as inventions that are known by an individual inventor, must be documented to be used effectively by the organization as an *intellectual asset*. After intellectual capital has been converted to an intellectual asset by writing it down, it may subsequently be converted into a legally protected *intellectual property* (IP) by (i) use of the patent system to obtain a patent that is a defensible exclusionary right or (ii) kept as a trade secret. Patent and trade secret intellectual property rights are a part of an enterprise's assets and can generally be leveraged in a number of ways to add value to the enterprise. IP is recognized as a large portion of the value of most enterprises today and in some cases represents essentially the sole value. The goal of this text is to assist the patent engineer or scientist to capture inventions, record them, and process them to create intellectual property (in the form of patents or trade secret protection) to optimally increase the value of the enterprise.

```
┌──────────┐  Document    ┌──────────┐  Legally    ┌──────────┐
│  Human   │  (Codify)    │Intellectual│ Protect    │Intellectual│
│Knowledge │ ──────────►  │  Assets   │ ──────────► │ Property  │
└──────────┘              └──────────┘             └──────────┘
```

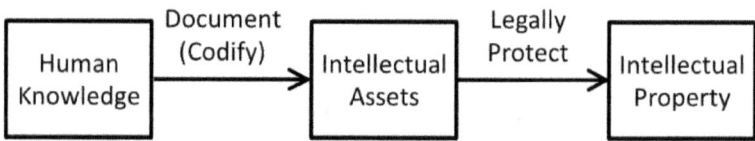

For companies operating in the US, the fast pace of innovation and the change in the US patent laws to a first-to-file system puts pressure on organizations to quickly harvest inventions and convert them into patent applications to be filed in the US Patent and Trademark Office (USPTO) with the expectation of receiving a patent grant. Time is limited for engineers, scientists, researchers, and investigators to prepare invention disclosures and begin the patent process. One solution is to employ skilled technical persons who are able to extract and document inventions and manage the invention review process. This includes facilitating a decision to apply for a patent, keep the invention as a trade secret, publish the invention, or put the invention on hold while waiting for further development.

To get the most out of this text, read and study the references to outside materials and do the exercises. Writing and speaking skills are essential. Above all, practice identifying inventions and describing them clearly and accurately in writing. You will most likely be called upon to make an oral presentation of the invention. If you need improvement in writing or speaking skills, focus on this first to be successful in this field.

Throughout this text the basic question is: "What Is the Invention?" When you can answer that question you can then document it and begin to create a valuable asset!

This text begins with a review of basic US patent law. Patent laws change frequently by court decisions and acts of Congress. Congress recently made a major overhaul to convert the US patent system into a first-to-file from a first-to-invent system. All patent applications filed after March 16, 2103, fall under the first-to-file system. It will take decades for the USPTO and the courts to interpret this new law. As a result, the patent law information in older revisions of this text may become out of date. A knowledgeable patent lawyer should be consulted on legal issues and changes to the law.

Section I

Basics

Patent engineers and scientists are not required to have a law degree. However, it is important to understand the basics of intellectual property law in order to support an intellectual property portfolio that optimizes value to the organization. This section outlines the basics of intellectual property law.

1. US and International Patent Law

US Patent Law

The basis for US patent law is the United States Constitution. Article 1, Section 8 reads, *The Congress shall have the power—*

to promote the Progress of Science and useful Arts, by securing for limited Times to Authors and Inventors the exclusive Right to their respective Writings and Discoveries. Congress has passed laws to grant patents for a limited number of 20 years from the date of the first patent application, with a possible extension for delays in the United States Patent and Trademark Office in processing an application.[1]

States grant patents to inventors or to other persons who own the invention, which may occur by virtue of assignment from the inventor to another person or by operation of law. When the term **state** is used in patent treaties, laws, and regulations, it normally means countries, such as the United States of America. The issued patent claims are generally enforceable only within the boundaries of the issuing state.[2] There is a provision for protecting products made abroad by a process patented in the US.[3] A patent applicant in one state may use its application to file corresponding applications in foreign states under international treaties. When this is done,

---

[1] Copyright is also protected by acts of Congress.

[2] In some cases, some claims may be infringed in one State and some claims may be infringed in another State. Telecommunications and e-commerce are examples of cross border activity. For example, the US Court of Appeals for the Federal Circuit enforced system claims for the Blackberry communications service that had a server in Canada because the effect of the system claims infringement was in the US. The claims of the US patents that were only infringed in Canada were not enforceable in the US. *NTP v. RIMM*, 418 F.3d 1282.

[3] 35 USC 271(g) pertains to infringement of products made outside of the US by a process patented in the US.

the new application in the foreign state receives the filing date of the original filing if the foreign application is performed in a timely manner. As a result, patents for an invention based on the same application may be granted and therefore enforceable in one or more states. The international process and reciprocal rights will be discussed in more detail later.

Until recently, the US granted a patent to the first person to invent a patentable idea, regardless of whether they were the first person to file a patent on their invention (a "first-to-invent" standard). Most of the rest of the world has historically granted a patent to the first to file a patentable invention such that it has been important for an inventor to quickly file their invention before others who may have come up with the same idea in parallel (a "first-to-file" standard). Effective September 16, 2011, the US patent law was amended by the America Invents Act (AIA) to transition to a first-to-file system fully implemented March 16, 2013. Patent applications, and applications dependent from patent applications filed prior to the effective date of March 16, 2013, are examined under the first-to-invent standard. Patent applications filed thereafter are examined under the first-to-file standard. As a result there was a transition period in which some USPTO rules applied to first-to-invent applications only. This manual applies to first-to-file practice only. Patent agents and attorneys have had to apply and navigate USPTO rules under both systems during the transition period.

For instance, a patent application filed before March 16, 2013, is examined by the USPTO under the first-to-invent legal standard, but a continuation-in-part application (new material added to the parent application) based on the pre-March 16 application may have the new material conceived after March 16 examined under the first-to-file system. This will be a topic ripe for litigation.

What we know about the new law is taken from its plain reading and its Congressional History. US federal courts will interpret the AIA in later court cases with unforeseeable results. This is a major change to the US patent law system, and its effects on innovation and intellectual property are yet to be discovered.

International Patent Law

Inventors and owners of the invention, often employers, may apply for a patent in foreign countries using the original US patent application if the same application is filed internationally under either the Patent Cooperation Treaty (PCT) or the Paris Convention within one year of the first filing date of the US patent application, including provisional patent applications. There are exceptions to this arrangement, notably Taiwan, which requires a direct filing before the invention is made public.

Most of the world's patent systems are first-to-file regimes. The first inventor to file a patent application is the party entitled to receive a patent grant, with exceptions. As a general rule, the applicant must not have derived the invention from another party, i.e., used another person's invention to apply for a patent grant. The applicant may use his foreign patent application date to establish the filing date. For example, a US patent application filed in the US, and subsequently timely filed in a foreign country under one of the treaties, is entitled to the original US filing date.

The Paris Convention provides for filing a foreign patent application(s) within one year of its original filing date. This treaty remains in effect today. It requires direct filing in each foreign country in which an application is to be filed. It is still a viable option if a US applicant only wants to file a few international applications (including Taiwan). There may be good reasons to select this international filing procedure, such as to accelerate examination and patent issuance in certain countries. In some cases patents first filed in non-English language countries—China, for example—result in a published application effectively being kept secret because of the language barrier.

The Patent Cooperation Treaty came about after the Treaty of Paris to allow consolidated international filing. It has some unified administrative procedures to simplify and streamline international patent procedures, including a single initial search report. In essence, an applicant may file a patent application in his host country and enter the international patent application process by filing a single PCT application specifying all of the countries in which he intends to seek patent protection. The PCT application will have one initial search by a selected examination authority and receive a single search report. The examination authority may be the USPTO or European Patent Office (EPO), for example. The applicant may respond to the search report with arguments and amend claims if appropriate. The application is then ready to enter the national examination phase of the individual countries he selected. It often happens that the applicant will drop the patent applications for some of the countries he selected in the initial PCT filing before entering the national phase in order to reduce expenses.

The European Patent Office is a consolidated patent application entity operating under the European Union that can issue a single European patent. This patent still must be nationalized in each European state in which it is to be enforced. There are similar consolidated examination entities in other regions of the world. The World Intellectual Property Organization (WIPO) can provide information on these entities. It is important to note that an EPO patent application may be filed either in English, German, or French. However, all foreign counterpart applications ultimately must be translated into the language of the country in which it is filed.

A new EU patent regime, *The European Unitary Patent System*, is proposed to be in effect by 2015. It is targeted to have a unitary patent covering multiple EU countries with a single translation and renewal fee, thereby saving costs. Alternatively, the patent owner can continue to use the present EPO, PCT, or individual state systems. The objective is to consolidate patent prosecution and maintenance and to reduce costs as a result. A single EU patent court is planned in parallel with courts in each country. Court procedures are still to be determined.

It is important to note that application length, including the number of claims, directly affects foreign filing costs. In many foreign countries a larger number of pages or claims, over pre-defined limits, increases filing fees. Translation costs must also be considered. Preparation of a US patent application that may be filed as a foreign counterpart should be done with all foreign filing costs in mind. Foreign filing and prosecution costs can be reduced by careful selection of an invention that meets the standards of patentable subject matter for the counterpart country (See WIPO). The preparation of the US application with an economy of text and claims that meets foreign standards can result in cost savings for the foreign counterpart application. There are commercial programs that will estimate the cost of foreign filings based on the number of pages, claims and country. Coordination with a patent agent or attorney in the counterpart country during the preparation of the US application to be foreign filed will increase the likelihood of issuance of a worthwhile and cost-effective foreign patent.

Technically, a patent office decision in one state is not binding on the patent office of another state. In practice, a foreign patent office's actions may have influence in a counterpart patent prosecution. The actions of a patent examiner may be viewed as those of an expert in the technical field and in some instances may be used to demonstrate to an examining patent office that there is allowable subject matter. Patents with foreign counterparts that are either licensed or enforced through litigation will be examined for compliance with the legal requirements of the issuing patent authority as well as for inconsistencies in describing the invention. Patent applicants that make inconsistent statements to different patent offices in different countries risk having the issued patents impaired in claim scope and enforceability. When prosecuting a patent in multiple countries, it is important to be consistent.

2.   Patentable Subject Matter

The US grants utility, design, and plant patents under Title 35 of the United States Code.

A *utility patent* is what is commonly understood to be a patent and generally provides exclusive rights to an invention for 20 years from the date of the patent filing. In order to reduce the initial filing expense and to make a timely filing under the first-to-file system, it is possible to file a *provisional patent application* with the United States Patent and Trademark Office, which can be less formal than a utility patent. The provisional patent filing establishes a filing date (important under a first-to-file standard) but must be converted to a more formal utility patent within one year of filing and prior to being examined by the USPTO and potentially granted. A utility patent application filed within one year of the filing date of the provisional application does not need to match the provisional application exactly, but common subject matter of both applications receives the earlier filing date of the provisional application.

Design patents are granted for a period of 14 years for ornamental features of an item.

Plant patents pertain to asexually reproduced plant varieties.

Utility Patents

Patent-eligible subject matter is set forth in Title 35 of the United States Code (USC) Section 101 (35 USC 101) as follows:

Whoever invents or discovers any new and useful process, machine, manufacture, or composition of matter, or any new and useful improvement thereof, may obtain a patent therefor, subject to the conditions and requirements of this title.

The Supreme Court has interpreted this section of the US Code by saying what is *not* patentable. The Court continues to define patentable subject matter as technology changes and new fields of industry and science evolve. Biotechnology, software, and the Internet have given rise to innovations not previously envisioned, and the Court has reacted to define patentable inventions in these new fields. The federal courts and ultimately the Supreme Court may change the interpretation of patent law in the future. Always ask a patent lawyer about patentable subject matter if you have any doubt.

Patent disputes are heard in federal district courts in each state. Patent appeals from these courts are heard exclusively by the Court of Appeals for the Federal Circuit (CAFC) in the District of Columbia. Decisions of the CAFC may be appealed to the Supreme Court. If it does not accept the case, the decision of the CAFC is upheld and is the settled law on the point.

The Supreme Court has said, *Congress intended statutory subject matter to "include anything under the sun made by man."*[4] The emphasis is on the qualification, **made by man**. Since this decision, patentable subject matter has been restricted by successive decisions by defining what is not patentable. But it remains that a critical element of patentable subject matter requires human intervention for invention. As a general rule the following are not patent eligible: 1) abstract idea, 2) law of nature, 3) natural phenomena, 4) mental process, 5) mathematical algorithms, and 6) scientific principles.

In comparison, the European Patent Office has said that the following are not patent eligible: 1) discoveries, scientific theories, and mathematical methods, 2) aesthetic creations, 3) schemes, rules, methods for performing mental acts, games, or doing business and programs for computers, 4) presentation of information, 5) those contrary to public

---

[4] *Diamond v. Diehr*, 450 US 175, 182 (1981)

order and morality, and 6) plant or animal varieties or essentially biological processes for the production of plants or animals.

The Supreme Court has provided guidelines as to patentable subject matter that carry forward to date. The guiding principle is that a human has to create something new. *The line between a patentable "process" and an unpatentable "principle" is not always clear. Both are conceptions of the mind, seen only by [their] effects when being executed or performed.*[5] The Supreme Court has decided a series of cases that are the guidelines for patent eligibility in the US. It decided, for example, that a calculation for alarm limits in connection with catalytic conversion of hydrocarbons was not patent eligible, primarily because the actual claim did not mention the chemical process. In contrast, *A physical and chemical process for curing synthetic rubber which includes the use of a mathematical formula and a programmed digital computer is patentable subject matter.*[6] As another example, the Court of Appeals for the Federal Circuit decided that an embedded digital watermark is an abstract idea that is therefore not patentable.[7] The following are some additional guiding cases.

Converting a number from one form to another without transforming an article in any manner has been deemed

---

[5] *Parker v. Flook*, 437 US 589

[6] *Diamond v. Diehr*, 450 US 175 (1981)

[7] *In re Nuitjen*, 500 F.3d 1346 (Fed, Cir. 2007)

unpatentable. Specifically, converting a binary number-coded decimal numeral to a pure binary that is not limited to specific use is not patentable.[8] It is equivalent to patenting an idea. If, however, the transformation would have caused some article to be changed or a process to be more effective, the conversion might have been patentable. Claiming the effect of the transformation might have resulted in patent-eligible subject matter. Describing the invention to capture a transformative act might have resulted in patent-eligible subject matter. The use of the conversion process in a computing system might have been patent eligible.

Novel manufacturing processes are in principle patent eligible. Chemical and assembly processes are examples. The use of computer-enabled process controls has been accepted as patent eligible. Joseph Marie Jacquard invented a machine-controlled weaving loom in 1801. He used a string of cards with recorded holes to operate patterns in looms. Arguably, it was the first machine to be controlled by programmed instructions and some say the precursor to machinery operated by computer instructions. The French government thought that the patent was so important that the government seized it for public use.

Instructions (software) to operate a computer are considered a process for patent purposes. The Supreme Court gave further guidance on patent eligibility for software in the *Bilski* decision.[9] The *Bilski* invention and claims are

---

[8] *Gottschalk v. Benson*, 409 US 63 (1972)

[9] *Bilski v. Kappos*, 130 S. Ct 3218 (2010), citing *Benson, Flook, and Diehr*

directed to hedging risks in commodity trading. In essence the claim was for a series of transactions between a broker and a purchaser to buy a commodity at a fixed price based on historical levels, identifying a producer-seller of the commodity, and initiating a series of sales or options transactions between the broker and producer-seller at a second fixed price such that the purchasers' and sellers' respective risk positions balance out. The Supreme Court decided that what *Bilski* claimed was an abstract idea and not patentable. The Court gave guidance by saying that *A claimed process is surely patent-eligible under § 101 if: (1) it is tied to a particular machine or apparatus, or (2) it transforms a particular article into a different state or thing.* The *Bilski* claims did not meet either of these criteria.

Courts have applied *Bilski* to find that (i) Internet viewing in exchange for watching advertising is not patentable,[10] (ii) an algorithm used in a garage-door opener is patentable,[11] and digital halftoning processes are patentable (because they are a *functional and palpable application in the field of computer technology*[12]).

As you document an invention that is implemented using software, ask what technical problem the invention

---

[10] *Ultramercial v. Hulu*, (C. D. Cal. August 13, 2010)

[11] *Chamberlin Group v. Lear Corp.* (N.D. Ill, Nov 24, 2010)

[12] *Research Corporation Technologies v. Microsoft*, No-2010-1037 (Fed. Cir. December 8, 2010)

solves and how it solves it to ensure it meets the limitations imposed by *Bilski.*

Laws of Nature are not patent eligible. Examples are: $E = MC^2$, $F = MA$, plants, and minerals. Electrical signals are not patent eligible because *A scientific principle, divorced from any tangible structure, can be rejected as not within the statutory classes.*[13] However, applying a law of nature in a novel way may be patent eligible. For example, Samuel Morse's invention of the telegraph was patent-eligible subject matter even though electromagnetism used by the telegraph was not.

Abstract Ideas are not patent eligible. The Supreme Court in its recent *Alice* decision held that claims for mitigating settlement risks in a financial exchange are not patent eligible.[14] The Court said that the claims at issue amounted to *nothing significantly more* than an instruction to apply an abstract idea of an intermediated settlement using some unspecified generic computer. Significantly, the decision applies to all types of judicial exception to patent eligibility. The Court went on to say that a novel and unobvious solution to a "technical problem" is not an abstract idea. The reliance on a "technical solution" is moving US patent law closer to the European Standard of the EPO that requires a technical

---

[13] *O'Reilly v. Morse*, 15 US (15 Howe) 62, 116 (1853)

[14] *Alice Corporation Pty. Ltd. v. CLS Bank International et al.*, slip op. No. 13-298, June 19, 2014 (Sup. Ct.)

solution to be patent eligible. It narrows the opportunity for patent-eligible protection.

In response to this decision the USPTO issued guidelines for patent examiners.[15] Previously there was separate guidance for product claims involving abstract ideas and process claims (Bilski guidance). This new single *Alice* standard may have a significant impact on biotechnology patents. The Alice two-step analysis is:

1. Does the claim recite an ineligible concept (natural phenomena, natural law, or abstract idea), and

2. If it does, does the claim recite sufficient additional elements to make the claim one to an *application* of the concept rather than to the concept itself?

Examples of abstract ideas include:

- Fundamental economic practices;

- Certain methods of organizing human activities;

- "[A]n idea itself; and

- Mathematical relationships and formulas.

Claim limitations that may qualify as *significantly more* include:

- Improvements to another technology or technical field;

---

[15] USPTO preliminary examination instructions in view of the Supreme Court decision in *Alice Corporation Pty. Ltd. v. CLS bank International et al.*, June 25, 2014

- Improvements to the functioning of the computer itself; and

- Meaningful limitations beyond generally linking the use of an abstract idea to a particular technological environment.

Limitations that are *not* enough to qualify as *significantly more* are:

- Adding the words "apply it" (or an equivalent) with an abstract idea, or mere instructions to implement an abstract idea on a computer; and

- Requiring no more than a generic computer to perform generic computer functions that are well understood, routine, and conventional activities previously known to the industry.

Natural Phenomena are not patent eligible. DNA is an example. But cDNA is patent eligible because it is man-made. A landmark Supreme Court decision, *AMP v. Myriad Genetics*,[16] decided this issue. The *Myriad* patent claims are composition of matter directed to several isolated human DNA molecules that represent the BRCA1 and BRCA2 genes. These gene mutations are associated with an increased risk of developing breast or ovarian cancer. *Myriad* created a cDNA molecule that holds the exact same information as the naturally occurring BRCA1/BRCA2 RNA. cDNA is chemically different from RNA and is commonly used in labs for testing.

---

[16] *Association for Molecular Pathology et al., v. Myriad Genetics, Inc. et al.,* 569 US 12at 8, 18 (2013)

cDNA is isolated from the cell and the living organism so that it can be tested and used in different ways. The decision held:

> *A naturally occurring DNA segment is a product of nature and not patent eligible merely because it has been isolated, but cDNA is patent eligible because it is not naturally occurring.*

While this decision is based on facts that pertain to biology, the concept that human activity is necessary for patent eligibility extends to all subject matter that aspires to a patent grant.

A new drug (pharmaceutical) or the use of it may be patentable. Likewise, diagnostic testing for a human or animal illness and conditions may be patent eligible. Administering a drug and measuring the body's reaction is not patent eligible. As an example, the relationship between concentrations of certain metabolites in the blood and the likelihood that a thiopurine drug dosage will prove effective or cause harm is not itself patentable. Claimed processes are not patentable unless they have additional features that provide practical assurances that the processes are genuine applications of those laws rather than patent claim drafting designed to monopolize the correlations. In the case of the relationship between certain metabolites in the blood and the effect of thiopurine: *The relation is a consequence of the ways in which thiopurine compounds are metabolized by the body—entirely natural processes. And so a patent that simply describes that relation sets forth a natural law.* [17] Administering a drug and determining the level of metabolite of that drug did not transform the correlation into patentable subject matter. However, if the drug changed the body's chemistry, it is patentable.

Recall that subject matter that is man-made is generally patent eligible. This is true even if the subject matter is alive. For example, genetically engineered bacteria used to clean up oil spills are patent eligible.[18] *It is clear from the Supreme Court decisions and opinion that the question of whether or not an invention embraces living matter is irrelevant to the issue of patentability. The test set down by the Court for patentable subject matter in this area is whether the living matter is the result of human intervention.*[19] Likewise, corn engineered to resist certain insects and pesticides is eligible.[20] In contrast, mixing nitrogen-fixing species of bacteria, called inoculants, which would infect several types of plants and enhance their ability to remove nitrogen from the air and incorporate it into the plants to form viral compounds, is not patentable subject matter.[21] There was no change in the bacteria. But there was a change in the infected plant. The changed plant may be patent eligible.

---

[17] *Mayo v. Prometheus*, Supt Ct 2012, favorably citing *Flook*

[18] *Diamond v. Chakrabarty*, 447 US 303 (1980)

[19] USPTO MPEP 2105

[20] *J.E.M. v. Pioneer*

[21] *Funk Bros.*, 333 US 127 (1948)

A method of inducing polyploidy in oysters by separating male and female oysters, inducing spawning, controlling the temperature of the eggs, fertilizing the eggs with sperm form zygotes, and applying hydrostatic pressure to the zygotes to induce polyploidy and then cultivating the polyploidy, is patent eligible. [22] The USPTO issued these guidelines for patent examination to implement the *Allen decision. Nonnaturally occurring, nonhuman multicellular living organisms, including animals, are patentable subject matter.*[23]

Bioinformatics is a cross between the use of algorithms, computational devices, software, and biology. If the biological material is changed by human intervention, the subject matter is probably patent eligible. If there is no change in composition of matter, the computational aspect of the invention must be the component that is patent eligible. Apply the *Bilski* test of whether the informatics 1) are tied to a particular machine or apparatus, or 2) transform a particular article into a different state.

The United States Patent and Trademark Office Manual of Patent Examining Procedure (MPEP) is the patent examiners' manual. It can be accessed through the USPTO Web site. The following is a summary of the patent eligibility guidelines. Always research the most recent changes for accuracy.

---

[22] *Ex Parte Allen,*

[23] US PTO O.G. 24, April 21, 1987

Factors Weighing Toward Patent Eligibility

- Recitation of a machine or transformation (either express or inherent)
- Machine or transformation is particular
- Machine or transformation meaningfully limits the execution of the steps
- Machine implements the claimed steps
- The article being transformed is particular
- The article undergoes a change of state or thing (e. g., objectively different function or use)
- The article being transformed is an object or substance
- The claim is directed toward **applying** a law of nature
  - The law of nature is practically applied
  - The application of the law of nature meaningfully limits the execution of the steps
- The claim is more than a mere statement of a concept
- The claim describes a particular solution to a problem to be solved
- The claim implements a concept in some tangible way
- The performance of the steps is observable and verifiable

Factors Weighing Against Patent Eligibility

- No recitation of a machine or transformation (either express or inherent)

- Insufficient recitation of a machine or transformation

- Involvement of machine, or transformation, with the steps is merely nominally, insignificantly, or tangentially related to the performance of the steps (e.g., data gathering) or merely recites a field in which the method is intended to be applied

- Machine is genetically recited such that it covers any machine capable of performing the claimed step(s)

- Machine is merely an object on which the method operates

- Transformation involves only a change in position or location of article

- "Article" is merely a general concept

- The claim is not directed to an application of law of nature
  - The claim would monopolize a natural force or patent a scientific fact; e.g., by claiming every mode of producing an effect of that law of nature
  - The law of nature is applied in a merely subjective determination
  - Law of nature is merely nominally, insignificantly, or tangentially related to the performance of the steps

33

- The claim is a mere statement of a general concept
- Use of the concept, as expressed in the method, would effectively grant a monopoly over the concept
- Both known and unknown uses of the concept are covered and can be performed through any existing or future-devised machinery, or even without any apparatus
- The claim only states a problem to be solved
- The general concept is disembodied
- The mechanism(s) by which the steps are implemented is subjective or imperceptible
- Basic economic practices or theories (e.g., hedging, insurance, financial transactions, marketing)
- Basic legal theories (e.g., contracts, dispute resolution, rules of law)
- Mathematical concepts (e.g., algorithms, spatial relationships, geometry).
- Mental Activity (e.g., forming a judgment, observation, evaluation, or opinion)
- Interpersonal interactions or relationships (e.g., conversing, dating)
- Teaching concepts (e.g., memorization, repetition)
- Human behavior (e.g., exercising, wearing clothing, following rules or instructions)
- Instructing how business should be conducted

Design Patents

Design patents are used in circumstances where the design feature is novel and valuable. Examples are shoes, consumer products such as the Dyson vacuum cleaners, Web sites, mobile phone cases, furniture, outdoor trash receptacles, park benches, and automobiles. The test for patent eligibility is whether the design is *ornamental* and not functional. Comparable patent protection exists in most industrial foreign countries. On the next page is an example of a Nike design patent.

Plant Patents

Asexually reproduced plants (except potatoes or other edible tuber reproduced plants) are patent eligible. [24] The USPTO Web site has a good explanation of patent eligibility requirements and inventorship for a plant patent. A utility patent may also be filed for plants, seeds, genes, etc. Additionally, protection for true breeding seed-reproduced plant varieties may be obtained through the Plant Variety Protection Office in Beltsville, Maryland.

---

[24] 35 USC 161

Inventions = Money

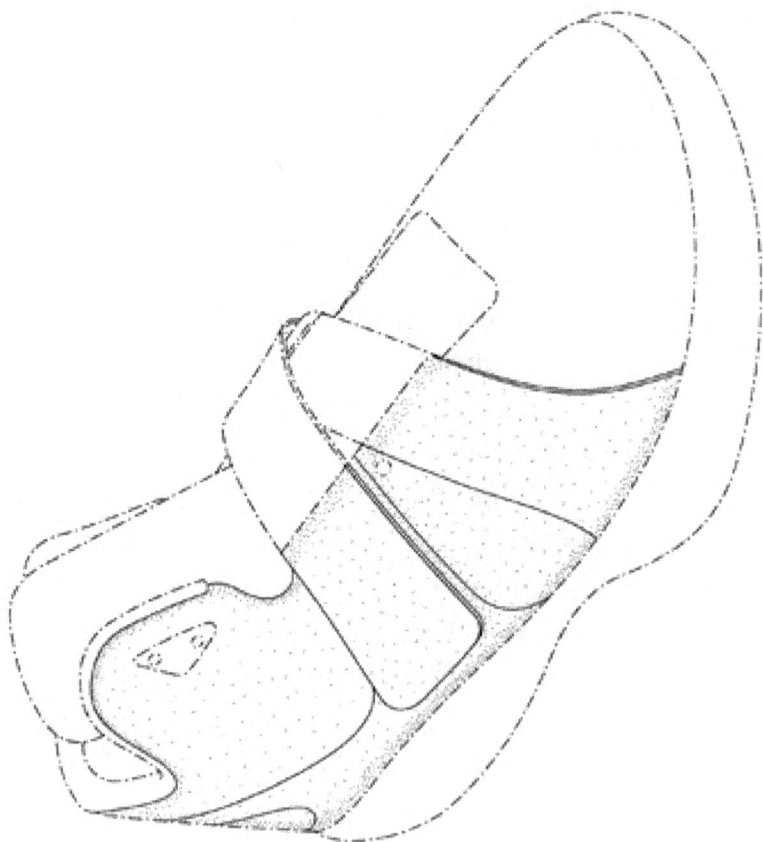

FIG. 1

The Monsanto soybean patents illustrate the value of plant patents. The US Supreme Court upheld Monsanto's genetically altered soybean seed patents for seeds that grow a plant resistant to the Roundup herbicide, itself a Monsanto product. The ruling prohibits the unauthorized use of patented self-replicating seeds, especially since the purchasers agreed not to do so. In contrast, many countries are hostile to patents on seeds, plants, and other botanicals.

An interesting question of patent eligibility is the in situ application of a chemical or biological agent to a plant to cause it to change. Is the man-made non-asexually altered plant patent eligible?

3. Novelty and Obviousness

Novelty

An invention must be novel in order to be patentable. Prompt filing of a patent application is critical under the new US systems to ensure novelty. The America Invents Act of 2011 changed the fundamentals of US patent law not only by moving to a first inventor system, but also by changing the test for novelty. The applicable section of the Code for novelty is 35 USC 102.[25] A patent rejection for lack of novelty under

---

[25] **§ 102. Conditions for patentability; novelty** (a) NOVELTY: PRIOR ART. – A person shall be entitled to a patent unless – (1) the claimed invention was patented, described in a printed publication, or in public use, on sale, or otherwise available to the public before the effective filing

35 USC 102 is often referred to as a "102 rejection." Under the new section 102, an invention is not novel if there has been public disclosure of the invention anywhere before an application is filed. The exception to this is disclosure made by the inventor, or someone who obtained the invention from the inventor, within one year of filing of the patent application as will be further discussed. Previously, only public disclosure in the US, or the worldwide publication of an invention, defeated its novelty. Now, under the AIA, public disclosure anywhere in the world defeats novelty. Because of this, prior art searching is more difficult and adds uncertainty to novelty.

The AIA defines the term *claimed invention* as *the subject matter defined by a claim in a patent or an application for a patent.*[26] Claims in a patent application as filed and amended, and those in the issued patent, are the *claimed invention*. Novelty of the amended claimed invention may be lost if prior art reads on it (i.e., all elements of the invention are present in the prior art) or if the amended claimed invention is encompassed by public disclosures. It is said that the prior art *anticipates* a *claimed invention* (i.e., defeats novelty so the claimed invention is not patent eligible) when the prior art fully describes the claimed invention. Claims are almost

----

date of the claimed invention; or (2) the claimed invention was described in a patent issued under section 151, or in an application for patent published under section 122(b), in which the patent or application, as the case may be, names another inventor and was effectively filed before the effective filing date of the claimed invention.

[26] AIA 2011 § 3(a)(2) (amending 35 USC § 100(j))

certain to change during the Patent and Trademark Office (PTO) prosecution and it is necessary to keep track of the amended claims during the PTO review (prosecution) process. Most foreign countries are *absolute novelty regimes* and allow for no grace period between disclosing an invention and filing it. Once an invention is disclosed, it is not considered novel in these countries. The safest course of action is to file a patent application before any public disclosure is made. It is absolutely necessary to file before public disclosure if reciprocal international patent applications are to be filed in foreign states.

The USPTO has taken a position that a claimed invention under the AIA encompasses not only the claims but also the specification description of the invention. The courts may ultimately differ on this interpretation. The term *claimed invention* may be interpreted differently in later court proceedings and could adversely affect a patent.

The AIA § 102 (a)(1) lists the acts that are considered public disclosure and defeat novelty if they occur before the effective filing date of the *claimed invention*. Printed publications and patents describing the invention defeat novelty. Also listed is the sale of the invention. These are carry-overs from the previous Code. New to the list is *public use* or *otherwise available to the public*. This language is similar to the definition of absolute novelty used by the European Patent Convention.[27] This new definition presents

---

[27] European Patent Convention Article 54(2). Any public invention disclosure before a patent application is filed defeats novelty.

a problem. Who is the *public*? Is a concealed part of an article made public when the article is sold? Is it possible that commercial actions such as manufacturing processes, and in some cases software, are not in public use are otherwise available to the public? Experimental use may or may not fall into this category. Courts will interpret which acts are public and the definition will change over time. The current best practice is to file a patent application before any public disclosure or sale of the invention to protect novelty. Always consult a patent attorney for guidance on what is public disclosure.

The AIA § 102(a)(2) lists patent documents that defeat novelty. These include a patent (§ 151) and the publication of an application for patent that name a different inventor (§ 122(b)). Published applications and patents do not automatically defeat novelty for a new patent if they have at least one inventor that is also an inventor of the claimed invention to be protected by the new patent. The work in general of an inventor of a *claimed invention* may not be prior art that defeats novelty for that claimed invention in some circumstances. The practical effect is that accurate naming of inventors may protect a patent application's novelty from a novelty challenge, particularly with respect to a patent or publication by a common inventor.

The AIA § 102 provides a one- (1) year grace period in which to file a US patent application after public disclosure of the invention by the inventor or those who directly or indirectly obtained the invention from the inventor(s).[28] It is necessary to keep track of inventor(s) and third-party public disclosures of the *claimed invention* to insure a timely patent application filing within the one-year grace period. The tem *claimed invention* is a term with specific meaning. (Claims will be discussed with patent contents in Chapter 5.) It is enough to know now that claims are the part of the patent that define its scope. They are often amended (changed) during the PTO examination process. At this time, it is unclear whether the claimed invention means those filed with the application or the claims ultimately allowed in an issued patent. Expect this issue to be resolved by subsequent legal proceedings. For now assume that claimed inventions means both claims in an application and as issued in a patent.

---

[28] **AIA § 102. Conditions for patentability; novelty** (b) EXCEPTIONS. – (1) DISCLOSURES MADE 1 YEAR OR LESS BEFORE THE EFFECTIVE FILING DATE OF THE CLAIMED INVETNION. – A disclosure made 1 year or less before the effective filing date of a claimed invention shall not be prior art to the claimed invention under subsection (a)(1) if – (A) the disclosure was made by the inventor or joint inventor or by another who obtained the subject matter disclosed directly or indirectly from the inventor or joint inventor; or (B) the subject matter disclosed had before such disclosure, been publicly disclosed by the inventor or another who obtained the subject matter disclosed directly or indirectly from the inventor or joint inventor.

Obviousness

Inventions that are obvious may not receive a patent grant.[29] Obviousness now is determined at the time that the patent application is filed. Previously it was at the time the invention was made, which was typically the date of conception. Obviousness is a legal determination and is hotly argued during prosecution and in litigation. The patent engineer should not try to determine obviousness but should record the invention and, if directed, search it for prior art and not comment on the whether the prior art may attract an obviousness rejection by a patent examiner or court proceedings. Case law on obviousness evolves and, if it is important, ask a patent attorney or agent the current state of the law.

It is important to have a basic understanding of the concept of obviousness as you identify patent-eligible inventions. The definition of obviousness is defined in the negative. It says what it is not. See the definition in part:

A patent for a claimed invention may not be obtained...if the differences between the claimed invention and prior art are

---

[29]**§ 103. Conditions for patentability; non-obvious subject matter.** A patent for a claimed invention may not be obtained, notwithstanding that the claimed invention is not identically disclosed as set forth in section 102, if the differences between the claimed invention and the prior art are such that the claimed invention as a whole would have been obvious before the effective filing date of the claimed invention to a person having ordinary skill in the art to which the claimed invention pertains. Patentability shall not be negated by the manner in which the invention was made.

such that the claimed invention as a whole would have been obvious before the effective filing date of the claimed invention to person of having ordinary skill in the art to which the claimed invention pertains.

The beginning of the analysis is to define a "person of ordinary skill in the art" (POSITA). The POSITA is a hypothetical person who is presumed to have known the relevant art at the time that the patent application was filed. Factors to be considered in determining the level of ordinary skill in the art may include: (1) type of problem encountered in the art; (2) prior art solutions to the problem; (3) rapidity with which innovations are made; (4) sophistication of the technology; and (5) educational level of active workers in the field.

The USPTO guidance to patent examiners provides rationales to reject a patent application claim in the MPEP Section 2141 is as follows:

(A) Combing prior art elements according to known methods to yield predictable results;

(B) Simple substitution of one known element for another to obtain predictable results;

(C) Use of known technique to improve similar devices (methods or products) in the same way;

(D) Applying a known technique to a known device (method or product) ready for improvement to yield predictable results;

(E) "Obvious to try"—choosing from a finite number of identified, predictable solutions, with a reasonable expectation of success;

(F) Known work in one field of endeavor may prompt variations of it for use in either the same field or a different one based on design incentives or other market forces if the variations are predictable to one of ordinary skill in the art; and

(G) Some teaching, suggestion, or motivation in the prior art that would have led one of ordinary skill to modify the prior art reference to combine prior art teachings to arrive at the claimed invention.

The USPTO goes on to outline the rebuttal expected from patent applicants to these rejections as follows:

(A) One of ordinary skill in the art could not have combined the claimed elements by known methods (e.g., due to technical difficulties);

(B) The elements in combination do not merely perform the function that each performs separately; or the results of the claimed combination were unexpected.

Patents are presumed to be valid but in litigation may be found to be invalid for a variety of reasons, including lack of novelty or obviousness under 102 and 103. The recent Supreme Court case on obviousness, *KSR*,[30] as it is known in the patent field, is thought to have made an obviousness

---

[30] 550 US 398 (2007)

challenge to a patent easier. Relying on the earlier *Deere* case, it reaffirmed that *the combination of familiar elements according to known methods is likely to be obvious when it does no more than yield predictable results*. The seminal Supreme Court case of *Graham v. Deere Co.*[31] instructs that the way to test for obviousness is to apply the facts as follow: 1) determine the scope and content of the prior art; 2) ascertain the differences between the claimed invention and the prior art; and 3) resolve the level of ordinary skill in the pertinent art. This suggests that a way to overcome an obviousness rejection is to show that the invention is not predictable. A practice tip is to describe an invention as having been made or discovered in an unexpected way, i.e., the results were not predictable.

The best way to understand the concept of obviousness is with examples. The USPTO has published a PowerPoint giving examples of obviousness. You can find it on the USPTO Web site under MPEP Section 2141. The patent engineer does not have to be concerned with obviousness except that it impacts the decision as to whether the invention merits preparation of a patent application. A practical way to address the issue of obviousness is to ask 1) did the invention solve an important problem, 2) is the inventor the first known person to invent, and 3) is the invention economically valuable? Considering the invention from the perspective of successful problem solving and documenting it accordingly

---

[31] 383 US 1 (1966)

will give the patent attorney ammunition to rebut an almost certain obviousness rejection.

4.   Statutory Bars (First-to-Invent)

Section 102 defines acts and events that are an absolute bar to a patent grant. Essentially, it constitutes public disclosure of the claimed invention before filing a patent application. The exception is that disclosure by an inventor or someone who received the information from an inventor is not a bar until one year after the disclosure. The most likely scenario is that an inventor presents a paper describing the invention at a symposium or there is a product demonstration at an industry meeting. Also, presentation to customers is disclosure. Basically, the inventor(s) needs to be questioned as to whom and under what circumstances products were demonstrated and papers or like made public. Also, if the inventor is part of a joint development project, disclosure to parties in the project is important to note, as will be discussed later. The patent engineer is responsible for collecting facts so that timely and sound decisions regarding protecting an invention can be made.

5.   Patent Structure: Background, Specification, Drawings, and Claims

A patent engineer does not draft an application and definitely should not independently prepare any section of a patent unless directed to do so by a patent attorney or agent. An axiom in patent practice is that anything written, unless protected by a privilege, is an outline for the author's deposition if there is litigation.[32] However, a patent engineer can collect the information needed to prepare a patent application and to that end should know the contents of an application.

A patent applicant is required to describe the invention so that a "person of ordinary skill in the art" can practice (replicate) the invention without undue experimentation, as described in 35 USC 112 below.

35 USC 112 Specification

The specification shall contain a written description of the invention, and of the manner and process of making and using it, in such full, clear, concise, and exact terms as to enable any person skilled in the art to which it pertains, or with which it is most nearly connected, to make and use the same, and shall set forth the best mode contemplated by the inventor of carrying out his invention.

The specification shall conclude with one or more claims particularly pointing out and distinctly claiming

---

[32] The communication between an attorney and client is privileged, as is the attorney's work product, and may not be disclosed without a court order or permission. However, communication between a patent agent and client is not privileged.

the subject matter which the applicant regards as his invention.

A claim may be written in independent or, if the nature of the case admits, in dependent or multiple dependent form.

Subject to the following paragraph, a claim in dependent form shall contain a reference to a claim previously set forth and then specify a further limitation of the subject matter claimed. A claim in dependent form shall be construed to incorporate by reference all the limitations of the claim to which it refers.

A claim in multiple dependent form shall contain a reference, in the alternative only, to more than one claim previously set forth and then specify a further limitation of the subject matter claimed. A multiple dependent claim shall not serve as a basis for any other multiple dependent claim. A multiple dependent claim shall be construed to incorporate by reference all the limitations of the particular claim in relation to which it is being considered.

An element in a claim for a combination may be expressed as a means or step for performing a specified function without the recital of structure, material, or acts in support thereof, and such claim shall be construed to cover the corresponding structure, material, or acts described in the specification and equivalents thereof.

In addition to describing the invention in general, the applicant must describe the best mode of practicing the invention. Prior law penalized failure to describe the best mode by allowing a court to declare it unenforceable for noncompliance with this requirement. The current law eliminates this penalty. Simply put, the patent must describe how the technology works so that a journeyman in the field can take the instructions in the patent and practice the invention, i.e., make or use the invention. Federal regulations provide further guidance on complying with 35 USC 112. Further, the USPTO Manual of Patent Examining Procedure has extensive guidelines for patent examiners in examination of applications and is a useful guide to a patent practitioner in preparing a patent application and should be referenced to understand the USPTO requirements for disclosure. There is a hierarchy of authority. The US Code (35 USC 112) is dominant, and the code of federal regulations (CFR) implementing the Code is subservient to it. The MPEP is an internal USPTO guideline and, while not law, is a reference used for making judgments as to compliance with the law and regulations.

Paragraph 1 of 35 USC 112 requires a written description of the invention. Patent practitioners have developed practices for complying with this requirement and the content of patent applications. A typical patent application starts with the field of the invention, background of the invention, a summary of the invention, brief description of the drawings, the detailed specification, and finally the claim(s). A closer look at the law (112, first paragraph) reveals that it does not require the typical contents just outlined, only the field of the invention, specification including drawings (if appropriate), and one or more claims. There is a school of thought to include only necessary portions of the applications. In litigation, licensing, and intellectual property mergers and acquisitions, all the words in a patent application have meaning. An unnecessarily lengthy specification is an opportunity for inconsistency. For example, summaries of the invention may not be complete because they are condensed and may lead to an argument that the claimed invention is narrow or different than claimed. Inconsistencies are opportunities for misinterpretation of the meaning of claims. Another example of writing more than is prudent is that a background section is prior art and an examiner may take all or some of it and combine with other art he found to make an obviousness rejection under 35 USC 103 (generally referred to as a "103 rejection").

The practice of limiting an application to the basic requirements may result in an application with a field of the invention of only a few lines, detailed description of the drawings, a written specification referring to the drawings, and the claims. Note that if the application is to be filed internationally, then the application may need to be broadened to meet the relevant foreign filing requirements. Care must be taken to use terms in an application consistently. The applicant can use his own definitions.

Otherwise, industry usage will most likely apply. And when claims are drafted, terms used in claims must be in the written specification or revealed in drawings. This is called antecedent basis for claim terms. Without support from the specification, the claim term is more likely to be interpreted by the court in litigation with uncertain outcome. An example of that follows.

Claims Define the Patent Grant

Claim interpretation (construction) is the foundation of evaluating a patent. Claims inform the public of the scope of the invention. Each claim is considered a separate invention. States (countries) determine the meaning of claims through patent office rules and court decisions. In the states with longer histories of patent law the courts have defined the meaning of terms by many of its decisions. For example, US court decisions have addressed the meaning of preamble terms in claims. Preamble terms that limit claim scope (breadth) are: "steps," "consisting of," "consisting essentially of," and "including." Likewise, the use of the term *means for* in the claim body, called a means-plus-function claim, may limit the claim to only that which is described in the specification and not equivalents. There are many more claims terms that US and older patent law regimes have defined. The result is that claims may be interpreted differently in different countries. There are algorithms and computer programs that can score US claims for use of proper claim language.[33]

The plain language of a claim may not be the actual scope of the claim. It is necessary to interpret a claim before a validity study is conducted or the claim is applied to an accused product or process to determine infringement. In the US legal system, the court that tries a patent infringement lawsuit will hold what is known as a Markman hearing to define the disputed claim terms. In the US, *The words of a claim are generally given their ordinary and customary meaning as understood by a person of ordinary skill in the art (POSITA) when read in the context of the specification and prosecution history.*[34] This is referred to as intrinsic evidence. If further evidence is needed to interpret the claim, the court may look to outside sources such as technical dictionaries, technical printed material such as treatises, textbooks, learned articles, and general dictionaries. This is extrinsic evidence.

The law of the state granting the patent determines claim interpretation and court decisions in that state. Universally, the first step is to understand the state of the art at the time of the invention. In the U.S. legal system a patent and its claim are written to be understood by a POSITA. In the EPO the claim is directed to a "skilled person." Essentially each state's patent system requires that the specification teach the

---

[33] For example, the US consultancy IPVision has a rule-based program to score claims for syntax and breadth.

[34] *Philips v. AWH Corp.* 415 F.3d 1303, 1313 (Fed. Cir. 2005)(en banc)

invention to a person with knowledge of the technology being described.

If the claim language is susceptible to different interpretations and it is unclear as to which is meant, then the specification is the next source of interpretation. A claim term means the same as it means in the specification of the patent. The technical term for this is that the claim term has an antecedent basis in the description of the invention (specification). This may include a written description and drawings, illustrations, diagrams, and other visual representation of the invention.

Although claim terms are generally given their ordinary meaning as would be understood by a "person of ordinary skill in the art" (or skilled person), a patentee can give terms a unique meaning by the way in which he describes them in the patent specification. In the US legal system the concept is that a patentee may be his own lexicographer. The EPO also allows a patentee to define terms that he uses in his claims. For example, when the term *semiconductor* is used in a patent specification and claim, it has a commonly understood meaning. If a class of semiconductors, such as a "light-emitting diode" (LED) is used in the specification or a claim term, the fact that it is a semiconductor may not be apparent to all readers. It may simply be understood to mean a light source with a given range of light spectrums. In this instance, the term *LED* would be understood in the way in which it is used in the claim and described in the specification. If it is used to describe a structure, then it might be understood to be describing a type of semiconductor. If its light properties are being claimed, then it may be understood as a light source. The patentee may explicitly define "LED" in the specification of the patent to ensure an accurate interpretation in the context of the invention.

A frequent question is who is a POSITA? A way to think of the person is one who is given a description of the invention in a patent application (including the written description, drawings and illustrations and claims) who then can practice it without undue experimentation. Examples are a code writer, production chemist, machinist, production engineer, and like technical personnel who implement designs, schema, or graphic interfaces and otherwise execute instruction for making a product or process.

Examples of Claim Interpretation

The interpretation of the term *space* in the claim below was key to an infringement case (see figure on p. 57):

1. I claim:

    An automotive catalytic converter, comprising:

    a porous ceramic cylinder,

    a resilient material wrapped around a portion of the exterior surface of the porous cylinder,

    a hollow cylinder,

    the porous ceramic cylinder wrapped with the resilient material inserted into the hollow cylinder to *space* the ceramic cylinder exterior surface from the interior surface of the hollow cylinder, and

the hollow cylinder compressed to hold the resilient material wrapped porous ceramic cylinder.

Intrinsic Evidence

Referring to the figure on page 57 from the actual US patent, assume that the patent specification describes the resilient material as a shock-absorbent mat (**13**) that acts as a cushion to protect the ceramic material (**7**) enclosed by the exterior cylinder (**31**) and that the cylinder is compressed at (**29**). Further assume that the patent specification describes the shock-absorbent mat (**13**) as being compressed by the cylinder (**31**) in the area (**29**) to hold the porous cylinder (**7**) in place to act as a shock absorber. Does the word *space* in the claim mean that the porous cylinder (**7**) had a space (air gap) between it and the interior of the hollow cylinder (**31**)? Or does the word *space* mean that the mat (**13**) filled the space between the porous cylinder (**7**) and the hollow cylinder (**31**)? The trial court deciding this issue said that *space* meant that there must be an air gap between the porous cylinder (**7**) and the hollow cylinder (**31**). The reasoning was that the plain meaning of the word *space* controlled and that there was no need to interpret it by reference to the drawings and the written description.

The correct way to interpret the claim is to look at the language of the specification and the referenced drawings and see how the converter is shown. If the court had done this, then it would have been clear that the resilient material (absorbent mat) (**13**) was in contact with the porous cylinder (**7**) and the interior wall of cylinder **31** at **29** and that it is impossible for there to be a gap between the resilient material (**13**) and the cylinder (**31**) because the porous cylinder (**7**) wrapped in the resilient material (**13**) would not have any support within cylinder **31**—and that was the point of the invention, to provide the porous cylinder (**7**) with a resilient support. The US Court of Appeals for the Federal Circuit may review the Court's interpretation of claim language.[35]

Since the patentee used the term *space* without further qualification, and the word is in dispute, the correct way to interpret the claim is to see if the patentee has defined it in the patent technical description, including the written description and the accompanying drawings. Let's assume that the patentee said, "the cylinder (**31**) is compressed at point **29** to compress resilient material **13** to hold porous cylinder **7** in place." Nothing is said about a space.

---

[35] *Phillips v. AWH Corporation*, 363 F.3d 1207, (CAFC, 2004) established the standards for interpreting US patent claims.

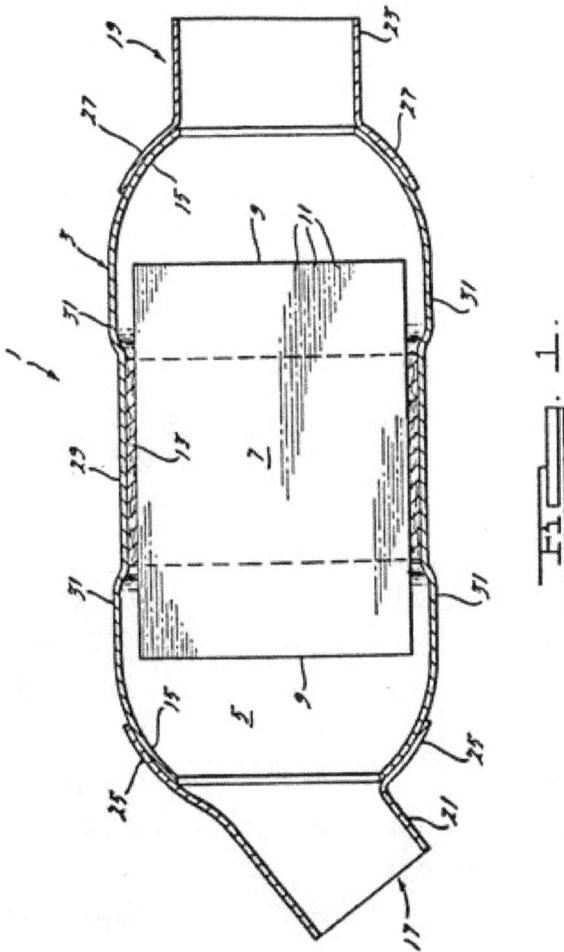

The specification is directed to a POSITA or "skilled person." Then the proper question is what that person would understand, not a judge. Looking at Figure 1 above, it is clear that cylinder **31** is reduced at point **29** to hold resilient material **13** by compressing it. Would it have been better if the patentee had said this and not used the term *to space* and instead used the term *compressively holding* in reference to resilient material **13**? This might have avoided the incorrect interpretation of the claim by the court. The choice of words in claims is important!

If the meaning of the term *space* is unclear to a POSITA or skilled person based on the claim alone, then the next step is to look at the patent's technical description to see if the meaning is further clarified. Assume that the patentee said that the resilient material (**13**) conforms to the shape of the porous cylinder (**7**) and that it will expand when it is heated and set into a new resilient shape. Furthermore, the catalytic converter assembly (**1**) will be used to remove toxic exhaust gas from an automotive engine and that temperatures when so used will be very high. And the catalytic converter when assembled will have a porous cylinder (**7**) wrapped in a resilient material (**13**) and inserted snugly into a cylinder (**31**) and the cylinder (**31**) compressed manually by a machine at point **29** to hold the combined porous cylinder (**7**) wrapped in the resilient mat (**13**). Taken as a whole, this describes the material expanding when heated to a new resilient shape and occupying all of the space between the porous cylinder outer circumference and the hollow cylinder interior wall. Therefore, there could not be any air gap or other space between surfaces according to this description of the invention.

There still may be a dispute over the meaning of the word *space* since an argument may be made that the actual dimensions of the components may allow for a space. Assume that when the patent application was being examined by the PTO that the applicant explained that when the assembled catalytic converter (**1**) was exposed to engine exhaust heat that the resilient material (**13**) described in the application would expand and fill all spaces between the porous cylinder (**7**) and the hollow cylinder (**31**) at point **29** because the material inherently expands into any open space. Therefore, there cannot be any space between the porous core (**7**) and the cylinder (**31**) when the catalytic converter (**1**) is used with an engine.

Assuming that this is true, the question remains: is there an empty *space* between the porous cylinder (**7**) and the hollow cylinder (**31**) before the exhaust gas heats the resilient mat (**13**)? If there is a space between the porous cylinder (**7**) and the hollow cylinder, (**31**) then the catalytic converter (**1**) may not infringe at this point because the catalytic converter (**1**) is not within the scope of the claim (infringed). Therefore, the manufactured product may not infringe the claim. But once the catalytic converter (**1**) is attached to an engine and exposed to exhaust gas heat and the resilient mat (**13**) expands and fills all spaces between the porous cylinder (**7**) and the hollow cylinder (**31**), then the absence of any gaps eliminates a possible interpretation that *space* means a gap.

Extrinsic Evidence

Since all of the intrinsic evidence has been examined and since the question of the meaning of the word *space* remains, extrinsic evidence [36] must be examined to answer the question of the meaning of *space*. Next, assume for this discussion that the manufacturer of the resilient material (**13**) has published a specification describing the materials characteristics. The materials description states that it will deform at 10 psi to fill all surrounding contiguous space whose dimensions are within 25 percent of the materials thickness.

The unanswered question is what pressure is applied to the combined cylinder (**7**) wrapped in the resilient material (**13**) when the hollow cylinder (**31**) is compressed at point **29**? If the hollow cylinder's (**31**) material and thickness are known, then the amount of pressure to deform it may be calculated. If the change in dimension of the resilient material before and after compression is measured, that may determine how much pressure was applied. Or if the weight of the porous cylinder (**7**) is known, then the force to hold it in place in the catalytic converter (**1**) may be calculated. Another approach may be to ask an expert in the field to testify as to the material's characteristics and how much pressure is applied when assembled in the catalytic converter (**1**), and if possible measure an assembled unit. He may also create an assembly

---

[36] Extrinsic evidence is information not in the patent document or the patent prosecution history during the prosecution of the patent application in the USPTO.

described in the patent and testify how much pressure he applied to get the same result as the claimed catalytic converter (**1**). All of these are examples of extrinsic evidence to interpret a claim that cannot be interpreted by intrinsic evidence alone.

Another example of claim interpretation is the *Saffran* case, in which judges on the Court of Appeals for the Federal Circuit differed as to essential claim terms.[37] It reversed a $500M judgment based on claim interpretation. The patent in issue is US 5,653,760 ('760) (See figure on page 64). The abstract describes the invention as follows:

> *The invention is designed to help restrain small structural or minor fracture fragments (**5**), and the macromolecules they produce (**8**) in specified compartment. The **device** is composed of a single sheet of material (**1**) that in its principle embodiment is supplied as a thin, pliable fabric that is flexible in three dimensions and is minimally porous to macromolecules. When the method if use contains the step of affixing a treating material (**12**) to the **device** prior to use, additional materials can be delivered directly and preferentially into [sic] specific compartments. Moreover, because the devices can be made of a soft fabric, a needle can be passed through the **device** and additional treating materials can be repeatedly injected*

---

[37] *Saffran v. Jonson & Johnson* (Fed. Cir. 2013)

*into and contained after the **device** has been deployed. The invention also permits delivery of energy (23) directly and specifically to the treated surface. The rate of repair can be further accelerated by the attachment of a treating material (12), either mechanically or by chemical bond (24), to one surface of the **device**.*

There were three terms construed (interpreted) by the court. For simplicity, the focus is on one claim (1) and term, "device." Examine claim 1 below.

Claim 1

1. A flexible fixation *device* for implantation into human or animal tissue to promote healing of a damaged tissue comprising:

a layer of flexible material that is minimally porous to macromolecules, said layer having a first and second major surface, the layer being capable of being shaped in three dimensions by manipulation by human hands,

the first major surface of the layer being adapted to be placed adjacent to the damaged tissue,

the second major surface of the layer being adapted to be placed opposite to the damaged tissue,

the layer having material *release means* for release of at least one treating material in a directional manner when said layer is placed adjacent to a damaged tissue,

the *device* being flexible in three dimensions by manipulation by human hands, and the *device* being capable of substantially restricting the through passage of at least one type of macromolecule therethrough [sic].

In discussing the claim, the court said, *To improve the treatment of such injuries, the '760 patent discloses "a unique method of fracture stabilization and a means to restrain interfragmentary [sic] macromolecules using a single, flexible minimally porous sheet." Id.col. 7 ll. 34–36. For purposes of the '760 patent, substances larger than about 500 daltons (e.g., proteins and many drugs) are considered macromolecules. Id. col. 8 ll. 3–6. The single-layered sheet serves as a selective barrier that blocks macromolecules and larger particles, such as tissue fragments and cells, yet contain micropores sized to allow free passage for small molecules (e.g., water). See id. col. 13 ll. 39–57. Other sheets might be designed to screen molecules according to properties such as ionic charge or hydrophobicity rather than size. Id. col. 8, 11. 15–24. Once selected and cut to the desired size and shape, the sheet (1) is wrapped around or affixed to the fracture site, for example, with staples (6), as shown below.*[38]

---

[38] *Id.*

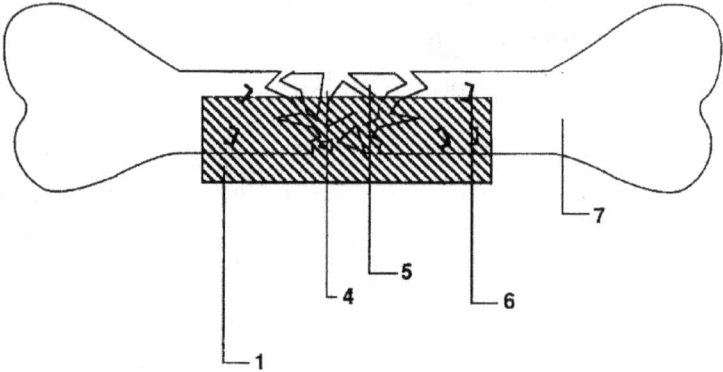

The question before the court was whether the term *device* should be interpreted to require a sheet. One judge said yes and one said no. Read the patent and then decide what the term *device* means. Also see if you can interpret the definition of the term *release means*. One judge said it only includes "hydrolyzable bonds" and another said it includes "chemical bonds and linkages." These examples demonstrate that claim writing with adequate support in the specification is difficult and subject to interpretation that may surprise.

6. Prior Art: Relevance and Searching

The object of searching for prior art is to discover if a claim is patentable as measured by 35 USC 102, 103; novelty and obviousness. [39] During the prosecution of a patent application, the patent examiner will conduct his or her search for prior art. In almost all prosecutions the examiner will reject one or more claims based on lack of novelty, a 102 reference, or obviousness, a 103 reference. The obviousness rejection may be based upon one or more pieces of art assembled to support the rejection. Searching prior to patent preparation and filing may narrow the risk of rejection but is unlikely to avoid it. Examiners have their own opinion as to the content and relevance of art. However, it may inform the invention owner as to whether a patent application is likely to succeed and thereby preserve resources by not proceeding if the search produces art that may be a bar. Alternatively, it may direct preparation of a patent application to likely patentable subject matter. If time permits, a prior art search is recommended before preparing a patent application.

Searching may be conducted at various stages of an invention's life. The pre-application searching of an invention disclosure (normally prepared by an inventor) is discussed above. It is usually referred to as a patentability search. Specialty firms are available to conduct these searches if you are not comfortable with conducting the search. Typically,

---

[39] Section 102 of the AIA defines prior art. It is public disclosure of an invention that is a bar a claim or claims.

the search is based on the invention disclosure. A complete and accurate invention disclosure is necessary for a competent search.

Applicants and their agents are not required to conduct a search before filing a patent application, but if you do, you must follow the USPTO disclosure requirements. Patent applicants and their agents are required to disclose to the USPTO art that is material to the examination of the patent application. Not doing so can invalidate a patent. Art discovered during searching that meets this criteria must be submitted to the USPTO during prosecution. A patent engineer should not make a legal judgment as to materiality. He should give the patent attorney or agent all of the art in his possession, whether it was gathered by him or by others. He should also ask the inventor(s) to give him art that they have that bears on the invention and give it to the attorney or agent. Let the attorney or agent make the legal decision as to whether to submit the art to the USPTO.

When patents are issued (granted) they are presumed valid. In layman's terms, the USPTO decided that the application met the standards to issue a patent. A patent may be invalidated if new art is discovered that the USPTO did not have or appreciate during the examination. Patent engineers familiar with art in a field are frequently called upon to help defeat extant (existing) patents. This may take the form of proceedings in the USPTO for re-examination or post-grant proceedings to invalidate claims, or in litigation when patents are asserted. This type of search is a validity, or invalidity, search. Both mean the same thing—looking for new art that is a 102, or in combination a 103, reference.

State-of-the-art searches survey patents by USPTO art classification, assignee (owner), inventor, etc. This may be used for information on competitors' patent portfolios as well as risks from third-party patents.

The patent engineer may also be asked to assess the risk of infringing a third party's patent(s). This is called a *freedom to operate* search and study. Relevant patents found during a search are examined to see if its claims read on an accused article of manufacture, process, or composition of matter (also design and plant patents). If there is an infringement risk, the patent(s) at issue are searched and studied for validity (prior art) and enforceability (usually failure to make required art disclosure or public disclosures to the USPTO during prosecution of the patent) and title (ownership). These are fact-driven legal issues.

The AIA has a post-grant challenge procedure allowing a patent to be challenged by a proceeding in the USPTO within nine months of issuance. A new aspect of patent practice will be to monitor newly issued patents as candidates for challenge. The USPTO publishes newly issued patents weekly in the Official Gazette each Tuesday.

Patents are grouped in the USPTO and foreign PTOs by classes and subclasses corresponding to a technology. This information appears on the front page of a patent. Examiners are likewise put in art groups that correspond to classes.

Unfortunately, the classification system is not perfect and sometimes a patent gets misclassified. It is hard to find relevant patents by a class search alone. Patent search firms are aware of this potential discrepancy and search accordingly. If you happen to be able to go to a USPTO office and meet with an examiner, he or she will help you outline classes and subclasses to search based on the invention disclosure. Frequently, he or she will have important art at hand and will share it with you, saving time and effort.

Patent portfolio mergers and acquisitions and patent licensing trigger prior art searching to determine the patent's vulnerability to either a 102 or 103 challenge. Note that practitioners use shorthand terms like 101, 102, and 103 rather than word descriptions. Even if the patent is valid, the strength of a potential attack is considered as a risk and part of the evaluation exercise.

Section II

What Is the Invention?

The most critical role of a patent engineer or scientist is to help the inventor define the core of the invention; what it is that is useful, novel, and not obvious. This section outlines the basics of defining an invention and what may and may not be patented.

7. Defining the Invention

Defining the invention is the critical first step in preparing an invention disclosure (ID). An accurate ID allows a patent searcher to search for prior art. As discussed previously, invention searching relies on an accurate description of the invention. Searching should occur after the ID is prepared so that when the invention disclosure is analyzed by a patent attorney or agent for preparation of a patent application the art found may be considered and will influence the determination of whether the invention is novel and if novel the anticipated claim coverage in a resulting patent. Otherwise time, effort, and legal fees are often wasted and the opportunity to create a valuable legal asset lost.

As an example, in Chapter 5 a catalytic converter claim construction was discussed. It is suggested that you read the patent and then decide, "what is the invention(s)?" (recalling that each patent claim is a separate invention). One way of describing the invention is: "a porous ceramic cylinder inside a hollow shell, the cylinder supported by a shock absorbing material positioned between the exterior of the cylinder and inside surface of the shell." Other features of the invention may be added to help a patent attorney draft further claims. This is desirable because, in the event that a court or the USPTO finds a claim invalid, other claims of differing scope may survive. What else is novel? Think about the process of manufacturing. Are the materials used in the converter novel? Consider the converter as it is installed on a vehicle connected to an engine. What are its operating characteristics?

An ID is the basis for a patent application. It is the foundation of the invention asset protection process. IDs (and patent specifications) must describe HOW an invention operates. A common mistake is to describe WHAT the invention does and not explain the details of the invention and how it works. The invention is described in detail in the application specification, which consists of written text often referring to drawings, figures, tables, screen shots, and other graphics. The invention must meet the disclosure standards of 35 USC 112, more fully discussed in Chapter 13. Patent claims define the invention and are the codification of the exclusionary right granted to the inventor. Patent claims are based on the invention description in the patent specification. That specification has its foundation in the invention disclosure.

Unfortunately not all patent claims are well written. We suggest that you don't draft or write patent claims. Even your drafts can be discovered in litigation and may negatively impact a court's interpretation of a claim, with adverse results. A trained patent attorney or agent should draft claims. Drafting claims is complicated and has very particular legal requirements. Improperly prepared patent claims have a negative impact if a patent is licensed, litigated, or sold. As an exercise, read patent claims in your technical field and if possible from your own organization.[40]

---

[40] The following are recommended claim-drafting practices to meet minimal format and structure standards. (a) Preamble: Be brief, use the broadest scope possible, and use the transitional term "comprising." Avoid using "having," "including," "consisting of," "consisting essentially of," or "steps." (b) Claim formats not to use: means-plus-function, Jepson, or multiple dependencies. Use Beauregard claims very carefully. (c) Claim terms not to use: "wherein," "whereby," "whereas" clause, or comparable terms of limitation. Do not use unnecessary limitations. (d) Antecedents: check for antecedent basis in use of claim terms in the specification.

Since it is recommended that patent agents or attorneys draft claims and the patent engineer define the invention to search it for patentability, the patent engineer's effort should be to 1) determine if the invention is likely to be patent eligible and 2) novel, insofar as is known. Ask the inventor what problem is being solved. Why is this solution new (novel), who else has solved this problem, and how did they do it? If the motive is not to solve a problem but instead is a discovery, ask why and how the invention or discovery was made. Was it an unexpected outcome? How is the invention used? What are its characteristics?

Ultimately the question of the invention's value to the enterprise is to be considered if a patent application is pursued. Said another way, "is the candle worth the game" or "if we get a patent, what is its value to the enterprise?" A well-prepared invention disclosure allows for 1) a preliminary novelty search, 2) prior art obstacles to be overcome, and 3) scoping of potential claim coverage. This information aids an informed decision on pursuing a patent.

8.   Processes and Methods

Processes and *methods* are steps for doing or making something. Most often, processes and methods that are simpler are commercially valuable. Examples of patented processes include making a beverage can from aluminum slugs using the steps of shaping and forming, operating a banking ATM enabled by software, a process to make coaxial cable, methods of petroleum refining, processes to create pharmaceutical formulations, processes for food preparation, and many other processes and methods that are useful, novel, and nonobvious. Note that the machines to do the steps may also be patent eligible in their own right.

The patented process to make a necked aluminum beverage can involves beginning with a slug and shaping by successive spinning steps, including repeated passes of shaping tools, to stretch the aluminum slug into a cylinder and then narrow the neck to a smaller diameter than the can body. This was considered useful, novel, and nonobvious.

The process for making a catalytic converter is also patent eligible. The patent discussed earlier describes not only the end product of the catalytic converter but a *process* of wrapping a porous ceramic cylinder with a resilient material, inserting the wrapped porous ceramic cylinder into a hollow shell, and reducing the shell to capture the wrapped cylinder by compression. A further process step is to apply heat to the assembly to cause the resilient material to expand in situ. What other process inventions are described in the patent?

In the case of Internet-based or software-based inventions, just as other inventions, the invention must fall into a category eligible for patent protection.[41] A Supreme Court decision set out two principles for software-enabled inventions: that the code must 1) be implemented on a

---

[41] 35 USC 101

special computer or 2) transform one thing to another.[42] The focus on defining an invention is not on the code but on what the code does and whether the result of using the code is novel. The following examples are meant to illustrate patent-eligible software-enabled inventions.

Using code to operate machines is not new. An eloquent example of a code performing a novel process is the previously discussed Jacquard loom invented in 1801 or thereabouts. There are many images of the invention online for those interested. The invention was to use connected punch cards to activate (or more accurately impede) knitting needles on a loom. It instructed the loom to weave and later knit. It was in fact using instructions to operate a machine.

Another example of an invention enabled by software is the Apple slide to unlock a mobile phone (US Patent No. 8,046,721). It unlocks the device by a gesture on an input and viewing screen and is enabled by code resident in the device. It may be defined as a user interface. Examine this patent and note the use of annotated flowcharts to describe the system architecture. Code is not used to describe the invention. A good practice is to avoid using code unless it is necessary to describe the invention.

An earlier touch-screen user-interface invention is the Citibank ATM touch-screen patent family. These Citibank patents enable a user to interact with an ATM display by touching the screen. The inventions were software enabled

---

[42] *Bilski v. Kappos*, 130 S. CT. 3218 (2010)

and described by annotated system architecture flowcharts.[43]

Patent applications that fall into the category of "business methods" are given special attention during examination by the PTO. These are typically ecommerce activities that include financial services. However, there is no clear definition of a business method invention. A good way to think about a business process implemented by software, which is the typical case, is to apply the tests for patent eligibility for software-enabled patents. The business process will probably not be implemented on a special computer; therefore the question is whether the process transforms one thing to another. In the case of touch screens, a tactile input is transformed into a command that operates a function such as unlocking a device or instructing an ATM to provide a service. Similarly, a consumer input into a telecommunication system may convert a currency value into another currency value to affect a funds transfer. In each instance there is a technical problem to be solved and software is used to implement the solution. These two examples may be patent eligible under 35 USC 101 if properly claimed.

A way to think about whether software enabled inventions are patent eligible is to ask, "what is the problem that is solved?" or "what is the advance made by the invention?" If

---

[43] Some of the patents are assigned to Transaction Technology, Inc., a Citibank technology development subsidiary.

the solution or advance is patent eligible, then describe the implementation of the invention by software. One example is the AT&T patents on link-listing of windows by bitmaps. This allows modern "windows display" on a computer interface. The invention was the concept that bitmaps define a body of information to be displayed and the pages defined as bitmaps can be linked for selected display. The original implementation was by electrical circuitry performing operational steps to define window topography, but it would now be accomplished with software. In electronic devices, steps once performed by electrical circuitry are now performed by software. A well-drafted claim might capture both an electronic circuit and software implementation of the invention.

9. Machines

The interaction of parts to create a result is a machine. Examples are rockets, robotic vacuum cleaners, wine cork pullers, bicycles, jet skis, electric razors, toasters, coffeemakers, weaving looms, beverage-can makers, fiber spinners, fork lifts, tractors, and components. Machines are embedded into everything from manufacturing processes to home appliances. A machine to make beverage cans was previously described. One aspect was to allow necking (narrowing) at the end of a tubular can. It resulted in a smaller, stronger end that used less aluminum and saved money.

Modern manufacturing incorporates logistics and product feedback in the integrated manufacturing process. The information interface that provides input and feedback may be patent eligible. Capturing the invention in these complex machines will require characterizing novel structures, processes, and controls affecting machine design, operation, and output. Even consumer feedback used as a control mechanism may be a patentable invention in some cases.

Recall the Jacquard loom, patentable as a machine in its physical embodiment together with the knowledge expressed in instructions in the control cards to operate the weaving needles and threads. Compare this to the combination of a computation element, such as a logic computer chip (machine), together with embedded instructions (computer code). Assuming they pass the tests of usefulness, novelty, and nonobviousness, these are both patent-eligible machines that may be claimed generally and specifically according to the specific set of embedded instructions.

10. Articles of Manufacture

Articles of manufacture (things) are patent eligible. Here are some examples of patent-eligible consumer products: robotic vacuum cleaners, fishing lures and tackle, coffeemakers, exercise equipment, golf clubs, golf balls, shoes, magnetic purse snaps, wine-bottle openers, and convection ovens. Look around you and identify novel articles and then take a moment to describe what is novel (new). Then do a quick search at the USPTO Web site for patents on the item. A Google patent search is also a simple step. This will help you recognize, visualize, and describe inventions.

For example, pop-top can openers are articles of manufacture. (Could one also be a machine?) Can openers were used to open beverage-can tops before pop-tops. Since this invention, there have been several variations of integrated can openers, including pre-punched surfaces to allow easy opening. An interesting example of invention is the shape of beverage cans. Note that the tops are usually necked (tapered). As previously discussed, this invention allowed the can top to be smaller and used less material, usually aluminum. The necked can shape was novel, as was the necking process. As an exercise, examine a beverage can and note what else is inventive.[44]

It is almost always true that a novel article of manufacture was made in a novel way, and if this is true, then the process of manufacturing the article is also patent eligible. Sometime a new material results in developing a new product and is patent eligible as a composition of matter. Consider the 3M™ sticky note an example. The 3M note is an article of manufacture, the process for making it by applying a new adhesive can be considered useful, novel, and nonobvious.

---

[44] Note that most soft-drink beverages such as Coke, Pepsi, and Dr Pepper protect the beverage ingredients as a trade secret.

11. Composition of Matter

Chemicals, compounds, combination of materials, and molecules are examples of compositions of matter. Basically anything that has a molecular structure that has been created or altered by human intervention is a patent-eligible composition of matter. Naturally occurring molecules are not. However, synthesized molecules replicating the function of a molecule in nature are patent eligible. An example is the compound Taxol produced in the bark of the yew tree. It is a cancer drug. The natural molecule is not patent eligible, but the synthesized molecules of Taxol were patented.

Synthetic fibers, plastics, ceramics, and battery materials are some examples of compositions that are being invented and improved upon. Organic material from nature, including the oceans, is being discovered and synthesized as patented compositions of matter for human use.

12. Improvements

An improvement to an existing invention, such as simplifying a process or method, is patent eligible. As an example, there have been successive, patented improvements in beverage-can pop-tops. Consumer products such as smartphones are constantly improved with those improvements patented. Software is updated frequently with new functionality. In each instance, the question to be answered for patent eligibility is the same: is it useful, novel, and nonobvious? Improvements may be more susceptible to a 103 challenge (obviousness) because they are based on an existing article, process, or composition. A good practice to prepare to overcome a 103 challenge is to describe the improvement as a new result or benefit and clearly explain the commercial benefit.

Section III

Preparing an Invention Disclosure

The invention disclosure forms the foundation for developing intellectual property. This section outlines the preparation of an invention disclosure.

13. Patentable Eligible Claims

As discussed in Chapter 2, the term *patent eligible* refers to the types of inventions and discoveries that may be the subject of a patent grant.[45] The Supreme Court (5-4 decision) has said, "Congress had intended patentable subject matter

---

[45] **35 USC 101 Inventions Patentable**—*Whoever invents or discovers any new and useful process, machine, manufacture, or composition of matter, or any new and useful improvement thereof, may obtain a patent therefor, subject to the conditions and requirements of this title.*

to include anything under the sun that is made by man."[46] The operative word is "made by man." Start with a clear understanding of "what is the invention." This is the basis of preparing an ID. You cannot document an invention unless you first know what it is. Ask what a human did that is useful, novel (new), nonobvious, and fits into the eligibility categories. If a human made a new technical contribution, it is probably patent eligible.

A caution: patent laws are in a state of flux with a new patent law fully effective on March 16, 2013, and the Supreme Court taking up patent appeals regularly. Patent eligibility is a hot topic for the Court and may be subject to change.

The question is how to make the initial decision on whether an invention is patent eligible. The ultimate decision as to patent eligibility should be made by a qualified patent attorney or agent, because this is a legal issue. However, the way an invention is described can and usually does make a difference in the decision. The emphasis should be on the human contribution. One way to describe an invention is by first visualizing it and then making a drawing or notes.

Recalling the catalytic converter invention, a drawing of the converter helps to visualize the actual implementation. Then ask questions: "Is the invention the shape of the shell? Is it the way that the shell is reduced with the converter wrapped

---

[46] *Diamond v. Chakrabarty et al.*, 447 US 303, 100 S. Ct. 2204

inside? Is it the application of a resilient mat placed between the catalyst and shell?" Maybe all of these are inventions.

Consider pop-top openers for beverage cans. Is the invention the idea that a tab presses against a weak spot on the can lid to break a seal? Is it the idea that a can lid can be weakened to permit entry? What are the components of the innovation that are useful, novel, and nonobvious? Note that later embodiments of pop-top inventions changed the tab structure and its fulcrum position on the lid, for example.

An invention may also be the recognition of a problem to be solved. In the medical field, the recognition that the absence of a protein causes a disease may be the point of novelty. In the case of a manufacturing process, the invention might be the recognition that the dwell time and temperature of a material such as foamed insulation in an extruder creates the desired characteristics. The B-29 aircraft was developed for high-altitude precision bombing in WWII to avoid enemy flak. When bombs were dropped from high altitude they missed the target. It was discovered that there are jet streams at high altitude that forced bombs off target. Discovering that jet-stream speed and direction information allows for adjustments to be made in bomb sighting was patent eligible.

14. Novelty and Nonobviousness

Claims define the invention. The term *claimed invention* is used in the AIA and in practice means the claims in the granted (issued) patent. This is not to be confused with the claims in the patent application as filed and amended during prosecution in the USPTO or foreign PTO. Since almost all claims are amended during prosecution, it is a dilemma as to how to make an initial judgment on the *claimed invention* since the final claims are not known until the USPTO grants the application.

In practice during the documentation, decision, and application phase of the patent engineer's management of the invention he or she can only approximate the claimed invention. One way to do this is to write a concise summary of the invention including all of the elements that are essential and nothing more. Put these elements in a grid and note the description of these elements in documents such as other patents, other patent applications, and publications as well as other sources of public disclosure. For example, using the catalytic converter discussed above, claim elements are put in a grid with columns for citations to publications in adjoining rows that are known and later discovered from searching.[47] Below is an example of how to record this data. If a patent attorney is involved in this process, he or she should be the one to record this information so that it is his

---

[47] Note that all of the examples are fictional.

or her work product and protected under the attorney's work product privilege.

Example of a Claim Grid

Catalytic Converter	US Patent 5,xxx,xxx	EPO Patent 123456	SAE Journal Vol. XV, 1980	SAE Exhibition, Dec. 1979
Porous Ceramic Cylinder	Col 3, ll 34-45 & Fig. 3	Paragraph 10 - 12 & Figs 7-8		
Flexible Mat				
Hollow Cylinder	Col 6, ll 5-10			
Ceramic Cylinder with Mat Around Its Circumference Inserted into the Hollow Cylinder			P. 23, Para 2	Sound Blasters Exhibit
Hollow Cylinder compressed to hold the Combination Porous Ceramic Cylinder and Mat				

If any one of the references in a column has corresponding data to every invention element, then it is possible that the invention is not new (subject to a "102 rejection" under 35 USC 102 for lack of novelty). The term used in patent practice is that the invention is *anticipated*. If a combination of references (two or more columns) have all of the elements, it is possible that the invention is obvious (subject to a "103 rejection" under 35 USC 103 for obviousness). A solution is to add elements that are not present in one or more references to a description of the invention. The added elements may make it new (novel) and nonobvious. Added claim elements generally result in a narrowing of the claim to avoid the art and make the narrowed invention new and arguably patentable.

Practice tip: Do not make judgments about what is patent eligible or new, especially in writing. If the patents are litigated your notes are an outline to your deposition and if it is an opinion on patent eligibility and novelty, it can impair the validity of the patent.

15. Statutory Bars (First-to-Invent)

Prior to the AIA certain acts were a bar to obtaining a patent. That has been replaced with a test for novelty to determine if the invention is barred from patenting. The first *inventor* to apply for a patent on a claimed invention is entitled to a patent on it if it is novel. An exception to this is that a person who derives the invention from another inventor or copies him is not entitled to an invention. Derivation will be discussed later.

The US now follows the European model of absolute novelty for a patent grant, but not exactly. For the purposes of sorting out whether to proceed with a patent application, define the claimed invention and see if it has been made public in any way.[48] Recall that most foreign countries are *absolute novelty regimes* and allow for no grace period between public disclosure of an invention and filing it. The AIA § 102 provides a one- (1) year grace period in which to file a US patent application after public disclosure of the invention by the inventor or those who directly or indirectly obtained the invention from the inventor(s).

---

[48] Note that disclosures made under confidentiality agreements or similar restricted circumstances are not generally considered public disclosures.

16. Inventorship and Ownership

Inventorship and ownership of an invention and a subsequent patent are intertwined. Patents are granted to an inventor, who is the initial owner. However, an invention, patent application, or patent may be assigned (transferred) to another party. These things are considered personal property and are treated as such by the law. They may be bought, sold, traded, loaned, or licensed, just as any other piece of personal property. If the inventor(s) is employed, the employer usually owns the invention with certain exceptions. In most organizations, the employee inventor signs an employment agreement or letter assigning his inventions and all intellectual property to the organization. Even if he does not overtly assign his invention rights, in most states the employer will own them as a matter of law. Even if the employer does not end up with title to the invention, it may have a *shop right* to practice the invention without compensation in certain instances.[49]

Each state provides for shop rights and invention ownership exemptions. Many US states have a statute that in general says that an invention not related to the employer, and made during the employee's own time and with his own resources, do not belong to the employer. It is always a good practice for the employee to make his invention known in

---

[49] A shop right is an implied license under which a firm may use a patented invention, invented by an employee who was working within the scope of their employment, using the firm's equipment, or inventing at the firm's expense.

general to his employer and get a written waiver to title for clarity. In practice, many employees do not do this because they are afraid of telling the employer that they have other interests.

If the employer is a university or research facility receiving funding from the US government, the Bayh-Dole Act determines ownership of the invention. It usually belongs to the employer with some exceptions. In certain circumstances the institution may waive the title to the invention, generally decided by the technology transfer office. In the situation where there is co-inventorship between a private entity and a US government–funded research institution, the result may be that title is held jointly and either party may license or use the invention without the consent of or accounting to the other.

A brief word about joint ownership of a patent: It is generally a major problem for the simple reason stated above, that either party may use or license the patent without approval of the co-owner and without accounting for royalties. It is like two persons owning an apartment building and each renting out apartments without being obligated to coordinate or share rent.

As a practical matter the patent engineer should record persons who may be inventors of the *claimed invention* and collect documentation supporting this initial indication of inventorship. The patent agent or attorney should make the final decision as to correct inventorship. Inventorship may change during prosecution when there are co-inventors because the inventorship is ultimately tied to the final *claimed invention* as defined in the issued patent claim(s). If one or more claims are abandoned or modified, such that the contributions of an original co-inventor are no longer included in the claimed invention, then that original co-inventor is no longer an inventor of the *claimed invention*. In the event that there is an honest mistake as to inventorship, it may be corrected during prosecution and after patent grant. As a practical matter, if a change in inventorship adversely affects ownership of a valuable patent, a dispute may result. In this instance, a good ID may resolve the dispute by proving inventorship.

Practice tip: Many people do not understand that inventorship is not a choice but is determined by who conceived the claimed invention. When people understand this distinction it is easier to ask for documentation to support their contribution to conception of the claimed invention. If there is no documentation, tell the patent agent or attorney this fact and let him interview the purported inventor to make the final decision. It is a legal matter determined by provable facts. Oral testimony without documentation for collaboration is a weak proof of inventorship. Documents trump oral testimony!

17. Duty to Disclose Prior Art

The patent applicant has a duty of disclosure, candor, and good faith in his dealing with the USPTO.[50] This duty extends to the inventor and patent application owner's agents, including patent agents and attorneys and possibly the patent engineer. Generally anyone in the patent process may be subject to this requirement.

The requirement is to disclose anything known to the applicant and his agents that is material to patentability.[51] This includes, for example, the results of prior art searches, references cited in corresponding foreign patent applications, conflicting statements made by the applicant in related patent applications, positions taken by the USPTO as to unpatentability of related applications, opposition to the USPTOs position, and statements made in litigations. Intentionally withholding this information from the USPTO is considered fraud and may have serious implications, including making a resulting patent unenforceable.

---

[50] 37 C.F.R. 1.56 *Duty to disclose information material to patentability.*

[51] Note that the applicant is required to disclose any known, material information but is not required to proactively conduct prior art searches or otherwise look for material information unless he is applying under accelerated prosecution procedures.

Practice tip: When interviewing inventors, ask if they have any information related to prior inventions by anyone else. Ask if they have published information about the invention in any way, including research papers, trade publication, grant requests, proposals to sell or license a product or service incorporating the invention, sales brochures, Web sites, and product specifications. Ask if the invention has been made public by anyone and, if so, whether that person obtained information about the invention from the inventor. Ask if they have discussed the invention orally and, if so, with whom and when. Ask if they have made a plant visit to view similar technology and if they signed an NDA or confidentiality agreement, or if there was such an agreement included in a sign-in form at the company site. Ask if they are a member of an industry standards group (for example, IEEE) or involved in a joint development of related technology. All of these may be sources of prior art that may be material and therefore disclosed to the USPTO.

Section IV

Invention Documentation

Accurate and complete documentation is critical in developing robust and defensible intellectual property. This section outlines a number of important best practices in invention documentation.

18. Technical Documentation

Patent engineers gather and document the initial information that describes the invention. This is used to search for prior art and to determine if the invention is to be pursued as either a trade secret or a patent application. If it is to be the basis for a patent application, the patent engineer should keep in mind what is needed to prepare the application. If the invention is kept as a trade secret, then, in addition to documenting the invention, the patent engineer must determine who has had access to the invention information and the systems and processes by which those people will be obligated to keep the invention a secret.

As previously discussed, a patent application must have a written description. [52] It describes "how" the invention operates. The description must be described in such detail as to instruct a "person of ordinary skill in the art" how to practice the invention without undue experimentation. The best mode of practicing the invention must also be disclosed. A caveat to this requirement is that failure to meet the best mode standard is no longer available as a defense to a patent's validity in an assertion. [53] Obviously, there is a contradiction since a patent applicant and his agent are required to disclose the best mode but if he does not comply, the patent may not be attacked in a patent assertion lawsuit.

---

[52] 35 USC § 282(3) (a) IN GENERAL—The specification shall contain a written description of the invention, and of the manner and process of making and using it, in such full, clear, concise, and exact terms as to enable any person skilled in the art to which it pertains, or with which it is most nearly connected, to make and use the same, and shall set forth the best mode contemplated by the inventor or joint inventor of carrying out the invention. (b) CONCLUSION—The specification shall conclude with one or more claims particularly pointing out and distinctly claiming the subject matter which [sic] the inventor or a joint inventor regards as the invention.

[53] 35 USC § 282(3) "failure to comply with—(A) any requirement of section 112, except that the failure to disclose the best mode shall not be a basis on which any claim of a patent may be canceled or held invalid or otherwise unenforceable."

As a consequence some applicants may decide to ignore the mandate to disclose best mode and risk the consequences of failing to meet the duty of disclosure to the USPTO to disclose the best mode. The decision as to what to disclose should be made by a competent patent agent or attorney. It is recommended that the patent engineer always record and disclose the best mode to the patent attorney or agent.[54]

A patent's written description also includes one or more claims. This is the legal description of the invention and claim drafting is a legal function. **Only a patent agent or attorney should draft claims.** Improperly drafted claims can seriously, negatively impact the value of a patent during a merger, acquisition, licensing, or litigation. Even draft claims discovered in litigation may be an admission that the claims do not cover what is intended. Although it is strongly recommended that the patent engineer does not write a claim, it is good practice to write a crisp description of the invention with all essential elements to be used as an outline in documenting the invention and as basis for a prior art search. Avoid saying that any particular aspect is the invention. Rather, say that this is the documentation of the work of a person (name him or them) who discovered or created an innovation that may be patentable.

A patent engineer may record an invention in any format that teaches it to a POSITA. The description should be a written document and supported by drawings, flowcharts,

---

[54] There are other legal theories that may be used to attack patents that do not have the best mode disclosed to the USPTO.

formulas, designs, tables, wave forms, mathematical notations, software code, etc. Note that in the case of a design patent, only a drawing (rendering) is necessary. Likewise, plant patents have unique requirements for documentation.[55] Seeds may also be recorded for separate IP protection.[56] A sample invention disclosure used for high-tech and software-enabled invention is shown in Appendix A. As much of the information as possible should be collected and recorded in this type of a document.

The catalytic converter discussed earlier is an example of an article that is manufactured and the process for making it. The drawing is representative of an embodiment of the invention but not a scaled drawing. The drawings only need to illustrate the invention. Multiple embodiments of an invention are possible and desirable. It is suggested that you read the 5,118,476 ('476) patent to better understand the information that the patent practitioner needs for the patent application.[57]

It is common for an invention to incorporate the article of manufacture and the process for making it. Include

---

[55] 37 CFR 1.163(a) "...the specification must contain as full and complete a botanical description as reasonably possible of the plant and the characteristics which distinguish that plant over known, related plants."

[56] Intellectual property protection for true breeding seed reproduced plant varieties is offered through the Plant Variety Protection Office in Beltsville, Maryland, which should be contacted for information regarding intellectual property protection for such crops.

[57] Go to www.uspto.gov, patent searches, or other patent-searching Web sites to find a copy of US Patent 5,118,476.

descriptions of both to accurately describe the invention(s) and to provide the patent practitioner with the opportunity to capture as many aspects of the inventions as practicable. In practice, the USPTO may restrict the application and force the applicant to select either article claims or manufacturing process claims. This may result in two or more patent applications and in turn two or more claims sets in separate applications (known as a divisional patent application).

19. Inventor Interviews

As discussed previously, inventorship is a matter of law. It is not elective. A party cannot name himself or others as an inventor if they do not meet the legal definition. The USPTO defines an inventor as one who contributes to the conception of the claimed invention. Inventions often involve co-inventors, each of whom contributes to the conception of at least one claim in a patent. Co-inventors may work remotely from one another and it is not necessary that an inventor reduce the invention to practice to be an inventor or co-inventor. The requirements to be considered an inventor or co-inventor are discussed in more detail in Appendix B.

It is important for the patent engineer to accurately determine both the inventorship and the ownership of the invention. If the inventor is working alone, he or she owns the invention and it is treated as intangible property. However, as previously discussed, if the inventor is employed, then the employer typically owns any resulting trade secrets or patents. Most employers require employees to explicitly assign all of their work-related intellectual property to the employer, including inventions and resulting patents. Recall also that federal law assigns title to inventions (and resulting patents) to non-profit organizations that receive federal funds with certain royalty sharing rights reserved to the inventor(s).

Because patents are property and the ownership originates with the inventor, accurately identifying the correct inventor(s) is critical to any subsequent transfers of title to a subsequent owner such as an employer. A mistake in identifying the correct inventor or owner may be fatal to the value of a patent since only the owner of an invention (whether a trade secret or patent) can license, assert against an infringer or thief, sell, or hypothecate to a lender.

Only a patent attorney or agent should make the determination as to who is the correct inventor, or co-inventor, of one or more claims in a patent. If a mistake is made, a patent may be corrected to accurately identify the inventors. The patent engineer has a role in identifying the inventor. As the invention disclosure is prepared, the patent engineer ideally collects the documents from the inventor that supports the invention's conception and, if appropriate, reduction to practice. Basically, document what he or she did and when. If the paper or electronic trail is sparse or non-existent, interview the inventor, if possible recording the interview for the record. Then transcribe the interview. It is best to have the interview witnessed or, if that is not possible, at least have the transcription witnessed. The reason for doing this is to preserve evidence if there is ever a challenge to inventorship. The patent engineer can and should tell the patent attorney or agent who he thinks are the inventors, and why, and give the attorney the supporting documentation. Documentation is essential for later proof of inventorship.

Patent ownership obviously determines who can enforce a patent. Unfortunately, patent enforcement actions have been lost because the party asserting the patent was determined not to be the owner. For example, Stanford University asserted a patent against Roche Molecular that was invented by a Stanford investigator, and therefore was presumed to be assigned to Stanford University as required under the Bayh-Dole Act. However, the Supreme Court in June 2011 found that Stanford did not own the patent in question because the inventor had previously assigned the invention and resulting patent to Cetus, and Roche subsequently bought Cetus, thereby owning the patent. The facts are complex and the decision should be read in full for a full appreciation of the facts and law. In essence, the Stanford investigator was found to have assigned his rights to the invention to Cetus during a visit to Cetus to conduct tests. He did this inadvertently by signing a standard form to access the Cetus facility and on the sign-in form assigning all inventions and rights related to the Cetus technology, including the rights of his Stanford patent, to Cetus. This took precedence over his assignment to Stanford University, as required under the Bayh-Dole Act. The lesson is that patent ownership is a matter of intangible property law and title follows ownership and must be addressed carefully.

The patent engineer should ask the inventor if he or she has visited other organizations and signed any documents regarding invention rights. If an investigator is about to go to another organization doing similar R&D, it is a good practice to ask that organization in advance if they require an assignment of IP rights or execution of a confidentiality agreement. If they do, have a patent lawyer pre-approve the agreement before the visit.

Technology employees change jobs and carry with them technical know-how and frequently the prior employer's confidential information. Sometime they also bring prior inventions. New employee or consultant inventors raise a red flag as to when the invention was made. If the inventor was employed by another organization when he or she conceived of the invention, then that organization typically owns the invention, at least in part. In this situation, the present employer's patent attorney should be informed and decide who owns the invention.

Practice tips: 1) always double-check a patent title starting with the correct inventor, 2) be suspicious of recently hired employees or consultants filing an invention disclosure, 3) always inquire if the inventor has visited an organization engaged in similar R&D, and 4) if a person claims to be an inventor but has no documentation to show this, interview persons who have knowledge of the person's contribution to the invention, document their input, and pass it along to the patent attorney for a decision on inventorship.

20. Inventors' and Agents' Knowledge of Prior Art

Applicants and their agents (typically patent agents and attorneys) are required to tell the USPTO about any information that may be material to the patent examiner during his or her examination of the application. This is known as the duty of disclosure and is set forth in the code of federal regulations, as outlined in more detail in Appendix C. A person subject to this duty of candor is not required to search for information. The duty only applies to information in their possession or under their control up until the patent is granted. Information to be disclosed is that which is *material to patentability*. This may include information on enablement, possible prior public uses, sales, offers for sale, derived knowledge, prior invention by another, inventorship conflicts, etc. As a practical matter, material information found after the patent grant may cause the patent owner or a third party to seek a re-examination of the patent based on the new art.

This is the type of information that often comes into the possession of applicants and his agents that may need to be disclosed to the USPTO:

- Art found in searches by applicant usually to determine if there is an opportunity to get claims allowed. Typically this is called a patent ability search and may also include state-of-the-art searches

- Foreign PTO search reports of counterpart applications

- Technical or sales information in the possession of the applicant or agent from

- Art cited by the USPTO in related applications, usually in a patent family

- Arguments made in related cases that are inconsistent with arguments mad in the subject applications, especially arguments that are in opposition to the position taken presently

- Validity issues of related patents in litigation

The operative words are "material to patentability." This is a legal decision, and it should be left to an attorney to decide if information is material. The patent engineer should collect all the information that bears on the invention and any public disclosure prior to filing an application and provide this to the attorney.

21. Searching Techniques

What is the invention? That is the question to be answered before searching for art that is either a 102 (novelty) or 103 (obviousness) reference bearing on the ability to get valuable claims in a patent. The search is looking for publications, including patents, that predate the subject patent's filing date. The publication date is most important, i.e., when was the information made public? Recall that it was suggested that a crisp description of the invention be prepared. The invention disclosure most likely will be the source of this description aided by interviews. Often this description will include diagrams, flowcharts, molecules, or graphic interface screen shots and like graphics. Since almost all searching is by computer and based on key words, it is important to identify key words necessary to the invention. Returning to the catalytic converter example, make a list of key words that are the basis for a prior art search. Try a simple search in the USPTO or Google patent databases and see what you find. Compare it to the patents cited by the examiner shown on the first page of the patent. In all probability it will not be exactly the same. Why? The examiner has collected art from multiple cases and searches and has a collection of patents and articles that may not be easy to find.

There are many reasons for variability in search results. The most common is that there is no standard language in many arts (technical fields as defined by the USPTO). An applicant may be his own lexicographer or use terms artfully. Also, terms used in the early phase of a technology may evolve, or there may be more than one way to describe a thing or process.

Patent searching is something of an art. Searchers who specialize in certain arts (technologies) become aware of art that is hard to find. The USPTO tries to accommodate searches by sorting all applications into classes and subclasses. However, art can be misclassified or properly classified in a different class such that search by art class or subclass alone will likely miss relevant patents. If you have access to an examiner, they will help with a search and even show art that they have accumulated.

An effective search technique once one or more relevant patents are identified is to search any prior art that was listed by those patents as well as any "cousin" patents.[58] By doing this, the web of related patents increases. There are very good tools provided by vendors to organize these type of search results along a timeline. [59] This is a good way to visualize parallel references and to determine publication dates.

---

[58] "Cousin" patents are patents that cite the same prior art as the patent in question. Patents that cite the same prior art are likely to be related in their inventions, and so the cousins of a relevant patent may be relevant as well.

[59] US consultancy IPVision has search tools that performs multi-layer searches and displays the results along a timeline.

Literature searches are also necessary. Any good library search tool works. A publication must be publicly accessible to be a suitable reference. Professional association publications such has the IEEE [60] and university papers, usually presented in journals and conferences, are good sources of publications. Also search conventions and conferences as well as Web sites to see when a product was offered for sale. Recall that an offer for sale may be a public disclosure. Also search funding agencies' databases like NIH for grant applications. A grant application may be a public disclosure.

After you have collected the references, use a claim grid (see Chapter 14) to compare each element of every invention element to the art to see if one or more references have all of the invention elements. A reference with all of the elements may have anticipated the invention and is a 102 (novelty) reference. If one or more references have all or most of the invention elements, then the invention may be obvious and is referred to as a 103 (obviousness) reference. Do not make a decision about patentability or make notes about your observations. Present the collected data either to the person in the enterprise who makes the decision on whether to apply for a patent or, better yet, to a patent attorney for his or her consideration as to whether valuable claims are likely to be issued in a patent grant.

---

[60] Institute of Electrical and Electronics Engineers

22. Re-invention and Double Patenting

In almost every large enterprise's patent portfolio there will be found duplicate claims in different patents. This is double patenting and may result in only the earliest claims being enforceable. It is a waste of resources and opportunities for a valuable exclusionary right. The larger and more dispersed the organization, the more likely it is that more than one inventor has solved the same problem and has an invention. There is no easy solution to this problem, but there are ways to reduce the wasted effort. A centralized invention disclosure and patent database is a good way to collect all inventions in one place. At least the persons having access to this information can serve as gatekeepers for new IDs. Another option is to internally (and confidentially) publish or otherwise make available relevant patent applications and patents from both third parties (public information) and the enterprise's own patent applications. This can be helpful in coordinating the IDs coming from separate R&D groups as a way to avoid duplication. A good practice is to catalog issued and pending claims by technology (USPTO art class is one way to catalog) as a master register of patent rights.

23. Invention Database

Another technique to manage the invention process is to keep a file of pending, rejected, abandoned, and issued patent claims. Likewise, a database of the state of the art, including the results of internal patent searches and all art cited by any patent office during prosecution, should be kept as a ready reference to decide if an invention may be patentable. A good way to organize the database is by USPTO classes and subclasses; then extract key phrases describing the invention by noun phrases and inventors. Place this data in a timeline to better see the evolution of the inventive activity. If noun phrases and inventors are displayed as a time progression, it's likely a pattern of invention will emerge that may aid in searches.

Section V

Patent Process

Invention disclosures (IDs) begin the patent process. The inventor, alone or with the help of the patent engineer or agent (attorney), documents the invention. The ID typically is sent to the inventor's supervisor and patent engineer or agent. An IP committee reviews the ID and decides how to proceed, which may include a number of options, including filing a provisional or utility patent right away, asking the inventor to flesh out the idea in more detail, abandoning the invention, publishing the invention to put it into the public domain, or keeping the invention a trade secret.

24. The IP Committee and Decision-Making

The IP committee is typically made up of senior employees or advisors with technical, marketing, and legal (patent) background in addition to the patent engineer or administrator. The committee's function is to make a business decision about what to do with inventions based on whether it believes the invention is novel and commercially valuable to the organization. As shown in the figure below, there are three paths for innovations: (i) protect the innovation by filing with the appropriate authority, in this case by filing a patent with the patent office,[61] (ii) protect the innovation as a trade secret, or (iii) abandon any protection for the innovation or put it into the public domain.

If the IP committee believes that the invention is novel and commercially valuable, it may decide to pursue a patent. If time permits, the invention is then searched for patentability and the committee revisits the ID with the search results. If relevant art is discovered in the search, the committee may request additional invention activity or further description of the invention. If the committee believes that valuable claims are likely to issue from a patent application of the invention, a patent attorney or agent prepares an application with the assistance of the inventor and patent engineer The applicant is not required to search for prior art before filing a patent application. However, the applicant (or their agent) is

---

[61] The IP committee may also look at innovations that can be trademarked or copyrighted.

required to disclose any material prior art that they are aware of to the USPTO. Not disclosing known material prior art to the USPTO is grounds for invalidating a patent even after it issues.

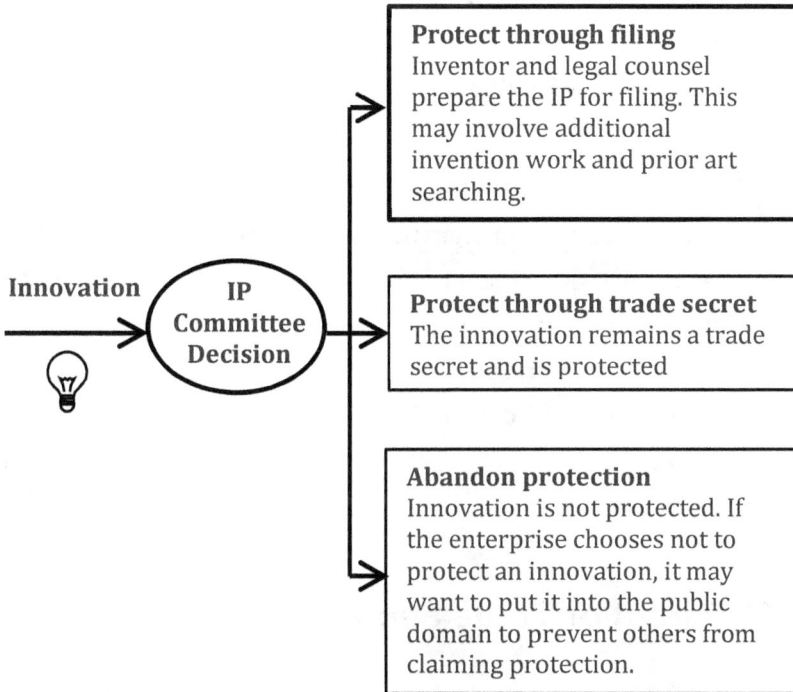

The IP committee may decide that trade secret protection of the invention is a better course of action. This is usually done if (i) the cost of obtaining and maintaining a patent is expected to exceed the economic benefit of the patent to the enterprise or (ii) the invention is very difficult to reverse engineer and the patent committee feels it is best to avoid disclosing the details of the invention publically, as required in a patent application. In these cases, the invention is generally marked as confidential and access to the invention is restricted.

The IP committee may decide that it is in the best interest of the organization neither to file a patent nor keep the invention as a trade secret. If the organization chooses to abandon an invention, and not protect it through patent or trade secret, it may choose to publish the invention in order to place it in the public domain so that it cannot be claimed by any other parties that may independently come up with the same innovation.

25. Patent or Trade Secret?

The patent engineer and IP committee that decide to protect an invention need to consider whether a patent or a trade secret is the better approach. There are trade-offs to both forms of invention protection.

Patents require the inventor to openly disclose details of the invention in the patent application, and the resulting patent (if granted) only provides protection for a finite period of time. [62] Even if there is a patent granted, the resulting claims may not provide valuable breadth of exclusionary rights. Patents also tend to be more expensive to prosecute and maintain than trade secrets. However, when issued, a patent provides robust legal protection even if others replicate the invention independently. Patents are enforceable against any party (other than a prior user).

Trade secrets can be maintained in perpetuity and can be valuable so long as they remain secret. However, once a trade secret is made public for any reason, its value is lost. This is true even if the trade secret is accidentally or even unlawfully disclosed. In these cases the person or entity that disclosed the trade secret is liable, but the innocent public that has received the trade secret information is not liable and can use the information as it likes. Trade secrets do not provide legal exclusivity of the invention. If other parties for any legal reason know the invention, such as if they independently developed the same or similar ideas, the owner of the trade secret may not exclude them from the making, selling, or use of the independently developed invention.

When considering whether to patent or create a trade secret, one should consider

1) How likely is it that the invention will be kept secret by the organization?

2) How easily can the invention be reverse engineered?

---

[62] Protection is granted for 20 years from the date of filing the patent application and its continuations and divisions.

3) Does the prior art make it difficult to get valuable patent claims?

If the invention can be kept secret and cannot be reverse engineered, then it is a candidate for trade secret protection. Manufacturing processes, for example, are often prime candidate for trade secrets. This can include things such as food recipes (with good examples being the soft drink formulas of Coke, Dr Pepper, and others), fireworks formulations (with proprietary mixtures for the propellants and pyrotechnics), and cosmetics formulations. If the prior art makes it difficult to get valuable claims, trade secret protection may be better even if lost in time. Conversely, it may be best to patent the invention if it is difficult to keep secret or strong patent claims may be available.

26. Assignment

Patents and trade secrets are intangible personal property. They can be licensed or assigned (sold) like any piece of property. [63] Assigned patents may be recorded with the USPTO, and the assignment will appear in the assignment records. If the assignment is recorded with the USPTO within three (3) months of the sale or mortgage, the assignee's title and lien status is superior to any intervening claims from the date of assignment to recording. Timely recording of patent assignment is important.

---

[63] Although it is possible to sell a trade secret, the sale is rarely made public.

Like any other piece of property, patents and patent applications may also be used to secure any financial transaction, such as a loan. The security interest may be recorded in the USPTO as described above, and it may also be recorded in the jurisdiction where the property resides (company location) and in the manner of recording security interest for the state and municipal entity (county, city, town).

27. Application Process

A provisional patent application only requires a written description of the invention, identification of the inventor, and filing fee. It does *not* require the inventor to specify the claims of the invention. Recall that the provisional patent filing establishes a filing date (important under a first-to-file standard) but must be converted to a more formal utility patent within one year of filing and prior to being examined by the USPTO and potentially granted.

A utility application must include a field of the invention, a written description, claims, identification of the inventor, an inventor oath, an abstract, and a filing fee.

A design patent application consists of a rendering of the design clearly showing the novel ornamental features.

Articles of manufacture may be eligible for both a utility and a design patent. However, a filing of either a utility or a design application on the same invention before the other is filed may be a patent bar in some jurisdictions. The filings should be coordinated.

Only a registered patent agent or attorney may file a US patent application and prosecute it in the USPTO. [64] The patent engineer's primary contribution to preparing a patent application is the preparation of a thorough ID to form the basis for a written description of the invention. The written description must give a full and clear disclosure of how to practice the invention without undue experimentation. [65] A hypothetical POSITA must understand the invention, and so must the patent examiner. The written description includes text and, if appropriate, illustrations, tables, and graphical representations to explain the invention. Brief examples follow.

Processes Including Software

Processes are described by steps to make something. Describe the steps sequentially and include the transformation of things or data during the process into a tangible result that is novel. The EU uses the term *technical solution* to define a patent-eligible invention. This also applies to software-enabled inventions. For instance, software and algorithms may process foreign exchange data for a transaction, resulting in a conversion rate and amount.

---

[64] One exception to this rule is that inventors may file a patent application themselves. This is referred to as a *pro se* filing.

[65] 35 USC 112, first paragraph

Software-enabled screen functions on mobile devices and phones may be patent eligible if they are transformative.

The conventional way to describe software-enabled inventions is to use annotated flowcharts. There is no specific requirement on how to disclose software, and it may be that additional code structure and snippets of code are needed. A complete set of source or object code is neither required nor recommend. The result of the functional steps that the code performs, usually expressed in flowchart form, is typically the invention.

Manufacturing processes may be patent eligible. Examples of patented manufacturing processes are found in food packaging, processing, and preservation; fibers; metals; recycled materials; petroleum refining; chemicals; cosmetics; data mining; data analytics; paints; coatings; and biological analysis (DNA and blood screening).

Compositions of Matter

Patent-eligible compositions of matter can include metallurgical compositions, chemical compounds, biological materials, etc. A metallurgical invention will typically include a description of the metals in portions and ideally any changed molecular structure. A compounded composition will typically recite the ingredients in ratios one to another. For example, formulations of cosmetics will have ingredients by ratios and maybe by weight of the total formula. Pharmaceuticals are typically described by molecular

117

structure. Biological materials may be described by molecular structure. Some examples of composition of matter inventions are paints, coatings, cleaning solutions, pharmaceuticals, carpeting, flooring, lubricants, fuels, food and beverages, and plastics.

Articles of Manufacture

An example of an article of manufacture is the catalytic converter previously discussed. The invention description consists of text referencing elements of drawings in various elevations, cross-sections, and perspectives showing the relationship of the elements of the invention. An engineering-level drawing is not required. Other examples of patent-eligible articles of invention are integrated can openers (pull tabs) on beverage cans, packaging (such as the twelve-pack cardboard can holder/dispenser), golf balls, golf clubs, luggage, mobile phones, electronic tablets, auto parts and assemblies, aircraft parts, robotic machines, household hardware, tools, watches, lighting, and magnetic handbag clasps. The USPTO classification system has a catalog of invention classes.

Designs

Design patents are described using pictures of the ornamental features of the invention. For example, see the Nike shoe design previously discussed. Further examples include outdoor furniture, indoor furniture, pottery, shoes, clothing, luggage, kitchen appliances, dishware, glassware, auto parts, bicycles, and boats.

Inventor

Initially the patent engineer will note who is likely an inventor as a result of the inventor preparing the ID and the patent engineer's interview(s) of him or her. An inventor is one who contributes to the conception of the invention described in one or more claims. Present patent law uses the termed *claimed invention* to more particularly identify claims as the expression of the invention. In the provisional patent application (PPA), claims are not required nor are they recommended. The submission of claims in a PPA may result in inconsistent claims filed later in a utility application, raising the possibility of unintended claim terms conflicts. Nonetheless, even in the case of a PPA filing, a good-faith effort is required to identify the inventor(s) to the extent possible. The only reference to potential claims in a PPA is the written description of the invention (the specification). When multiple people contribute to a patent application description, it may result that the initial named inventors are not the ultimate inventors of the claims in a patent, as claims likely will change during prosecution of the application in the USPTO. The patent attorney or agent is responsible for making the decision as to who the ultimate inventors are of the *claimed invention*. This is a fact-based legal decision. Only inventors of the final claims should be listed as the final inventors of the claimed invention. If all of the claims contributed by an individual inventor are rejected, they are no longer an inventor of the claimed invention, even if they contributed to the specification of the overall patent. If any claim has been amended during prosecution in the USPTO, and after the USPTO allows the final claims in the application, ask the patent attorney or agent to determine if inventorship should be corrected.

Preparing the Provisional Patent Application

The PPA written description must meet the standards of disclosure. [66] It must teach a POSITA how to practice the invention. Often a PPA captures the invention right after conception and before reduction to practice. Nonetheless, the disclosure must be complete to support subsequent claims filed in a utility patent application. This is difficult to achieve and survive later challenges. A practical way to document the invention as effectively as possible is to write a very brief description of the core invention(s) in a few sentences, identifying what is useful, novel, and nonobvious, but not in

---

[66] *Id.*

claim form. Use this as an outline for the more comprehensive written description and drawings.

Preparing the Utility Patent Application

When practitioners refer to patent applications they generally mean a utility patent application. This convention will be used in this text. The application is required to have a field of the invention, written description, claims, and abstract, plus the formalities of an oath and fee. The invention disclosure prepared by the patent engineer is the foundation for the written description and used to identify the inventors for the inventor's oath.

A preferred technique for preparing a patent application is to draft the broadest claim first, taking into account the invention disclosure and prior art. A patent applicant may only claim what is both disclosed in the application and not described in the prior art. By drafting the broadest claim first, the boundaries of the invention and prior art are established. One way to think of the claim boundary is to draw a circle defining the invention and one for the prior art. The circles may touch but not overlap.

The written specification and drawings enable (i.e., teach) the invention. Terms used in claims rely on the written specification and drawings for definition. If terms used in claims are explicitly defined in the written specification of the patent, they are said to have an "antecedent basis" in the specification. If there is no antecedent basis, then extrinsic

121

evidence is used to define the terms in a patent claim. It is crucial to use terms accurately in the application and not to use more than one term to describe an element, action, process, or any other aspect of the invention. Consistent usage of terms is critical to ensure clarity of meaning in a claim and avoid legal debates about what is specifically claimed. A good way to avoid duplicate definitions of claim terms is to create a numbered list of terms used and ensure they are explicitly defined in the specification and used consistently.

Each drawing, flowchart, table, or other graphical display of information is listed in the section "Description of the Drawings." The illustrations are numbered as Figures 1 forward in sequence. It sometimes occurs that an illustration is either a subset of another or is later inserted. In these instances, figures may be numbered as subsets, such as Fig. 1-A, or Fig. 1-1. Elements in the written specification refer to corresponding elements in the figures. Elements that are to be described in each figure should be numbered and should begin with the figure number. They need not be sequential. For instance, in Figure 1, the first element may be 102, and the next element may be 104. It is a good practice to use even numbers to allow for flexibility in case an additional element needs to be added and described. Once an element is numbered, that number is not changed even if used in another drawing. For instance, if element 104 appears in Figure 2, it is still 104.

Each word in a patent has meaning and, when a patent is enforced or licensed, its written description, drawings, and claims are closely scrutinized. There is a school of practice to be concise as a way to avoid duplication and unintended interpretations. If the application is foreign-filed, brevity can also help reduce foreign filing and prosecution fees as well as translation costs.

When patents are asserted, courts often end up interpreting patent specifications and claims, including the meanings of terms. A patent agent or attorney familiar with case law can draft claims with precise language to avoid misinterpretation by the courts. An example of problematic language in a specification is the usage of the word "embodiment" in association with an example of an invention. A court has interpreted the use of "embodiment" to mean only the embodiment(s) described in the invention, and not all possible embodiments. This limited the scope of the claims in the invention to the specific example(s) described in the patent specification. Now some patent agent and attorneys avoid the use of "embodiment" and use "example" instead. When drafting a patent, it is important to use specific terms that have specific meanings in the eyes of the courts.

Some patent practitioners continue the practice of including a background section in a patent application. The USPTO has taken the position that art disclosed in a background section is prior art and may be combined with a separate piece of art to reject a claim based on 103 obviousness. Including a background section is an unnecessary risk. If a background section is included in a patent, it must be carefully prepared. Similarly, a summary of the invention section must be carefully prepared if it is to be included. Courts may use such a section to limit the scope of claims to what is described in the summary or any discrepancies between the summary, and the written specification or drawings may result in ambiguity in term or claim interpretation.

The claims are included at the end of the patent and define the invention. It is critical that the claims are drafted precisely. The quality of the claim draftsmanship has the largest impact on the patent value, and claims should be drafted by a very experienced patent attorney. As a guideline, avoid the following terms in a claim preamble: including, consisting of, consisting essentially of, steps, and methods. Likewise, avoid these words in the claim text: wherein, whereas, and whereby. Also avoid words that approximate values or parameters if possible. Precision is best! If you are interested in claim drafting and interpretation, there are many treatises on this subject.

Prosecuting a Patent Application

After the application has been filed and all formalities met, the application is processed and assigned to an "art unit" at the PTO based on the subject matter. Each art unit has a different expertise and processing time based on the patent application backlog. If the examiner determines that the claims in the patent application describe more than one invention, he or she may require a restriction forcing the applicant to elect a subset of the claims to be prosecuted in the application. In this case, the application is effectively split into two or more different applications and the claims that were not part of the subset selected need to be filed separately in one or more divisional patents (requiring additional patent application fees). The examiner reviews the application for compliance with other disclosure requirements and conducts a prior art search to determine if the claims are useful, novel, and nonobvious. The examiner may accept and allow the claims as written but this is a rarity. Normally the claims will be rejected on one or more grounds in an "office action." The rejections may be for ineligible patent subject matter (101), lack of novelty (102), obviousness (103), or inadequate disclosure (112). The applicant can respond to the office action by responding with an argument (i.e., an explanation of why the rejection is unwarranted) or by amending (changing) the claims (or disclosure errors) to overcome the rejection. Note that the claims may be amended during the patent prosecution but no new description of the invention may be added to the written specification after the application is filed. The examiner can accept or reject the applicant arguments or claims amendments or search further if he or she feels that additional prior art can be found to reject the claims.

During the patent prosecution, the applicant can request an oral interview with the patent examiner, either in person or by telephone conference. Normally this type of interview is granted and can be useful in clarifying any misperceptions, exploring differences, and reaching agreement on allowable invention claims. It is important to avoid a written dialogue with the examiner if possible since recorded concessions and statements made by the applicant during prosecution can be used to restrict the scope of issued (granted) claims later. If no agreement is reached after the first office action and any associated interviews, the examiner can issue a "final office action" allowing the applicant only one more reply (argument or claim amendments). If, after this final reply, no agreement is reached, the applicant can file a request of continued examination or appeal to the US Patent Trial and Appeal Board. After the board's final ruling, further appeal is possible in federal court.

Third Party Art

The PTO publishes patent applications 18 months after filing (from first application) unless requested not to do so. If the inventor elects to pursue only US patent rights early in the prosecution, they can elect to delay the publication of their patent until issuance. Note that delay in publication can avoid alerting competitors to an inventor's activity. This is particularly desirable in some cases because the AIA allows for third parties (often competitors) to submit prior art applicable to a pending patent application to be considered by the examiner if timely filed, making a successful patent prosecution more difficult for the inventor.

Derivation

Patents may not be filed on inventions that were derived from another party. The AIA has added a new right and procedure in the US to prevent a party from claiming an invention that was derived from another party's invention. The EU has a similar process. This is done through a trial proceeding to determine the original invention activity and the misappropriation of that invention based on solid evidence. As will be discussed in detail in the next section, good invention documentation, proof of access to the invention by the alleged thief, and proof of a duty to protect the secrecy of the invention are all important elements of proof of derivation.

28. Maintenance

After a patent is granted periodic maintenance payments are necessary to keep the patent active. This applies to US and most foreign patents. Besides generating revenue for governments, the maintenance payments force patent owners to decide whether it is economical to keep the patent enforceable. Maintenance payments in the US are made 3.5 years, 7.5 years, and 11.5 years after the date of grant.[67]

---

[67] The fees change. As of this publication date the fees in US dollars for large entities/ small entities/ micro entities are as follows: 3.5 years— $1,600/$800/$400; 7.5 years—$3,600/$1,800/$900; and 11.5 years— $7,400/$3,700/$1,850. There is a grace period, although late fees apply.

29. Post-Grant Proceedings

A granted patent may still be amended by its owner or challenged by others in the USPTO. A patent owner can correct patent errors such as inventorship via a supplemental proceeding. The owner can also request patent re-issuance to adjust claims and make technical, non-substantive corrections. The owner can also petition to have a patent re-examined on the basis of new art (so that the art is considered in the prosecution of the patent and is less likely to be used by others to later challenge the patent validity). These are ways to strengthen a patent for licensing, litigation, and sale.

Other parties may challenge a granted patent's validity in post-grant USPTO proceedings that include a post-grant review initiated within nine months of patent grant and re-examination. Any basis for invalidating a patent may be used in the post-grant review, including ineligible subject matter (101), lack of novelty (102), obviousness (103), defects in the written disclosure (112), wrong inventor, inaccurate ownership, and equitable issues. After the nine months have elapsed and the opportunity to initiate a post-grant proceeding has passed, the remaining avenue for challenge is a re-examination based only on prior art that proves lack of novelty (102) or obviates the invention (103). Post-grant reviews are often used by litigation counsel to stay parallel patent litigation in which patent validity is at issue.[68]

---

[68] It is an interesting question as to what happens if there are simultaneous court and USPTO post-grant proceedings concerning patent validity and the court decides patent validity issue one way and the USPTO another. In a recent case, the decision favored the USPTO's decision for a procedural reason. No doubt there will be further CAFC interpretation of the relationship between court and USPTO conflicting post-grant decisions and perhaps involvement by the Supreme Court. The AIA's new provisions will be hotly litigated for decades.

Section VI

Management

It's important to implement systems and processes that optimize the value of IP protection in the context of organizational objectives. IP protection costs money, and the careful management of the IP protection process is key in realizing an optimal return on that investment. This section outlines best practices for the management of the overall IP protection process.

Most IP law firms are set up to provide a full range of IP management services, including prior art searches, writing of the specification and the claims, filing patents, responding to office actions, paying maintenance fees, and maintaining a docket that shows the current status of all of an organization's pending and issued patents. Allowing a single law firm to manage all of these IP logistics can often be the best solution for an organization. However, active involvement from the organization's management team, generally represented by the IP committee, is still always required to ensure that the IP protection is aligned with, and valuable to, the organization's overall objectives. The organization must also maintain internal systems and processes that support the protection and use of its IP.

30. Process Management Tools

The IP docket is the primary tool used to manage intellectual property. This is essentially a list of the patents filed by an organization and generally includes, among other things, the status of the patent (e.g., pending, issued, or abandoned) and any outstanding actions required together with their due dates (often bar dates). Outstanding actions might include response to an office action, payment of fees, or filing of supplemental material. Usually an organization's IP law firm maintains the docket and informs the organization when action is required. It is important for the organization management and the patent committee to review the docket on a regular basis to ensure that it is aligned with the corporate objectives. Failure to review the IP docket on a regular basis is a critical mistake in IP management. An organization should request regular docket reports from its IP law firm or the organization may choose to manage its own docket. There are online docket services that enable an organization to effectively and efficiently manage their own docket. In addition to providing the management and IP committee with immediate access to the current status of all patents, the approach of managing its own docket (in place of having its IP law firm do it) provides the organization with the flexibility to assign different resources to different patents to optimize the return on its investment and the quality of the portfolio. A simple example of this is that the organization may want to have a third-party expert perform the prior art search on a specific patent related to that expert's area of expertise.

Prior art searching tools can be as straightforward as public online databases, such as the one available on the patent and trademark Web site, or proprietary databases that might be leveraged by a law firm or independent search entity. They can also include more sophisticated tools, such as those developed by IPVision and others that analyze the inter-relationships and quality of prior art. It is generally not a good approach to run an automated prior art search that returns a large number of documents (e.g., patents) to be considered, unless automated triage is also used to recommend a limited number of documents that is reasonable for manual review. The filing entity has the duty to disclose to the patent office all information known to be material to patentability but is penalized for "hiding" relevant prior art by citing a large number of prior art documents such that the most relevant documents are not readily evident to the examiner. In the eyes of the patent office, the filing entity is aware of all the prior art that it has collected and reviewed during the prosecution, so collecting thousands of documents in the prior art search requires that all of those documents be reviewed and only the relevant ones submitted with the filing, which can be a prohibitively expensive exercise.

Patent strategy software and online tools exist for both prosecution and litigation. Online tools can be used, for example, to assess the relationships of patents to one another through citations. This can help understand the strength and age of a patent portfolio for a specific company or the relationships between the patent portfolios of two or more companies. In developing a patent portfolio, it can help in assessing potential partners or competitors in the space. More recent innovations in patent assessment tools include rule-based systems for automatically evaluating the general breadth and strength of claims in a patent or patent portfolio. Of course, a tool is generally only as good as the skill of the person using it. The key to the successful use of any of these tools is the experience and personal attention of the IP team.

31. Documentation for Defense

Documentation is a critical component of invention, independent of whether intellectual property protection is sought. Intellectual property laws are generally based on a "first-to-file" system. Under this "first-to-file" system, documentation demonstrating the actual invention date is less important in asserting priority than it used to be in the previous "first-to-invent" system used in the United States.

However, documentation of systems, processes, and ideas remains very important from a defensive perspective.

The America Invents Act expanded the "prior user rights defense" to include all methods or processes. What this means is that an individual (or an entity that controls, is controlled by, or is under common control) can escape liability for patent infringement if the patented subject matter was commercially used by the entity in the United States at least one year before the effective filing date or first disclosure of the patented invention. Commercial use includes internal commercial use or an arm's-length transfer of the final end product of such commercial use.

To use the prior user rights defense, the alleged infringer must demonstrate that they performed or directed the performance of the commercial use of the asserted IP for more than a year prior to the first disclosure of the patented invention. For this reason, it is important to document all methods and processes being used in preparation for a potential prior use defense. The defense is only applicable to an entity or person who has been using the asserted method or process itself for more than a year. The right to assert the defense cannot be licensed or transferred, except through the good-faith transfer of part or all of the business in which the commercial use exists.

The prior user defense may typically only be asserted at the sites where the commercial use was present before the effective filing date of the claimed invention. An exception to this occurs when there is an assignment or transfer of the business in which the commercial use exists, in which case the prior user defense may be used at the sites where commercial use was present on the assignment or transfer date if that date is later than the effective filing date of the claimed invention.

Abandonment of commercial use of the patented subject matter ends the individual or entity's ability to assert the prior use defense unless, of course, the commercial use was resumed more than one year before the effective filing date or first disclosure.

Even if all the other factors are satisfied, the prior user rights defense is not applicable to IP that was owned by, or subject to assignment to, a university or technology transfer organization at the time the invention was made. This applies specifically to IP owned by or assigned to technology transfer organizations that have a primary objective of facilitating the commercialization of technologies developed by universities.

32. Derivatives

The AIA and EU patent laws are based on the first inventor to file a patent application. To avoid the theft of an idea and its patenting by a party who is not the inventor, both legal systems prohibit a person who derives the invention from the inventor from receiving a patent.

The America Invents Act provides for a derivation proceeding between two patent applicants before the USPTO Patent Trial and Appeal Board to determine who is the true inventor and entitled to the patent. The true inventor must file a petition for a derivation proceeding within one year of the first publication of the invention.

The petition for a derivation proceeding must show:

1) the petitioner's invention is the same or substantially the same and is not patentability distinct from the earlier applicant's invention;

2) the invention was derived from the inventor on the petitioner's application;

3) the earlier application was filed without the inventor's authorization; and

4) the construction of the petitioner's claims accurately reflects the true invention.

To show that the invention was derived from the petitioner requires documentary proof supported by testimony. This proof is essential to get a proceeding initiated. The patent engineer plays an essential role in this proceeding by his or her documentation of the invention and accompanying records that can accurately identify the inventor, invention, and circumstances of the invention. It is also crucial to document that the party who took the invention had access to it. Confidentiality agreements and visitor logs are sources of proof for access and duty to protect the invention from disclosure.

Another scenario that can lead to a contest over ownership of an invention is joint R&D projects and joint ventures. Innovation projects with other organizations that expose inventors to the work of other participants can lead to cross-pollination of ideas, which is usually the object of the cooperation. However, this comingling of creative ideas may create an issue of inventorship and in turn ownership. This is an area ripe for claims of derivation. Recall that a person who conceives of an invention that is expressed as a claim in a patent is an inventor. Likewise, a person who contributes to an invention expressed as a claim is a co-inventor. And inventors who are employees generally owe a duty to assign inventions to their employer either by their employment contract or operation of law.[69] Note that true co-inventors cannot derive an invention from the other inventor. A person who claims that a patent applicant derived his invention from him is essentially making a claim of ownership for himself or his employer.

When structuring a cooperative project such as a joint venture, it is recommended that the parties put agreements in place up front to specifically identify ownership of resulting inventions and their subsequent use. A common compromise is to agree that any inventions, including patents, will be jointly owned. However, joint ownership of patents is problematic since either party may practice the

---

[69] If there is no employment agreement, then state law applies and the duty to assign can be verified by consulting with an intellectual property attorney licensed in the state in question.

invention, including licensing and sale of its interest to a third party, without accounting to the other owner. Essentially, neither party controls the technology. If there must be joint ownership of resulting patents and related technology, a comprehensive ownership and management agreement is highly recommended. Think of two parties owning an apartment building without agreeing on rents, tenants, and maintenance. It is unworkable. This is similar to ill-defined joint IP ownership.

The joint research project must document the inventions produced by it and inventors. The participants should periodically (no less than quarterly) submit invention disclosures to the project managers, who should review and resolve any conflicts over inventorship. This may prevent disputes over derivation if one party files a patent application without the permission or knowledge of the other. Invention documentation is essential to resolve inventorship and ownership disputes at this level and later.

33. Use of Confidentiality Agreements

Confidentiality agreements, sometimes called confidential disclosure agreements (CDAs), nondisclosure agreements (NDAs), or secrecy agreements, are contracts entered into by two or more parties in which one or more of the parties agree that certain types of information disclosed by one party to the other will remain confidential. These agreements are often put in place to evaluate business opportunities or conduct ongoing business between two or more parties in which trade secrets or inventive activities are involved. Confidentiality agreements must be used properly to maintain the integrity of an intellectual property portfolio.

A fundamental objective of putting confidentiality agreements in place when sharing sensitive technical or commercial information is to establish a legal obligation for the receiving party to not disclose or use the confidential information in ways that are outside the permissible scope defined in the agreement. If the terms of the confidentiality agreement are breached, the injured party has cause to seek injunctive and monetary damages. This allows the disclosing party to share confidential information for specific purposes that are anticipated to have a benefit to their organization, while mitigating the risk that the confidential information will be used in ways that hurt their organization.

Even in situations where a confidentiality agreement does not serve other aspects of a business relationship, one should be used to ensure the integrity of intellectual property rights. Under the laws of most countries, including the US, the public disclosure of an invention (e.g., disclosure in the absence of a confidentiality agreement) can be deemed a forfeiture of the rights to patent that invention. Properly drafted confidentiality agreements can prevent accidental and undesired forfeiture of patent rights.

It is generally important to define exactly what information can and cannot be disclosed and how confidential information may be used.

The confidentiality agreement should classify nondisclosure information as confidential. This may or may not include things such as technical, marketing, pricing, business planning, and other information, know-how, prototypes, drawings, software, tools, systems, specifications or data regarding programs, platforms, systems, business models, products, and company operations. Any information that passes between two parties can fall under a confidentiality agreement and it is generally best to specifically define in advance what type of shared information will be considered confidential and any exceptions. It is common, for example, to provide exceptions for information that the recipient can demonstrate was already in their possession prior to receipt from the discloser, information that becomes known to the public through no fault of the recipient, information that is legally disclosed to the recipient from a third party, or information that is independently created by the recipient.

The confidentiality agreement may also limit each party's use of the confidential information. In many cases, for example, the confidential information is disclosed purely to evaluate a potential business deal and may not be used by the recipient otherwise in their business. It should be noted here that this creates a liability for the recipient, who may be excluded from leveraging information that they receive under a confidentiality agreement that they may have otherwise discovered or invented themselves. This negative impact of receiving confidential information is sometimes referred to as "IP contamination."

Because of the responsibilities and potential liabilities associated with signing a confidentiality agreement, is important to specify both (i) the time period during which disclosures will be made and (ii) the time period during which confidentiality of the information is to be maintained. In situations where the agreement is anticipated to be in place for the foreseeable future, it is generally best to retain a fixed term of the agreement and include provisions for renewal of the agreement when that term expires, upon the consent of both parties. This approach facilitates an ongoing agreement but removes the unnecessary and inappropriate liability associated with an open-ended agreement.

If trade secrets are exchanged, the trade secrets should be designated as **RESTRICTED MATERIAL** and the terms of confidentiality extended until its owners make the information public.

In anticipation of the confidentiality agreement expiring at some point, confidentiality agreements should contain a provision stating that no implied license to the technology or information is to be granted to the recipient, that all tangible embodiments of the information should be returned upon termination of the agreement, and that no copies shall be retained by the recipient.

It is typical under a confidentiality agreement for a party to handle confidential information received by the other party in the same way that it treats its own confidential information. Therefore, it is prudent when signing a confidentiality agreement to understand the standards by which the other party or parties handle confidential information. If there are any concerns about the standards by which a party maintains confidential information, those standards may be written explicitly into the confidentiality agreement.

Overall, it is important that a confidentiality agreement be as specific as possible about the status and type of information shared, the period of time over which information may be shared and must be kept confidential, and other material terms associated with sharing of confidential information. The agreement should optimize the ability to meet business objectives while protecting confidential information and avoiding IP contamination.

34. Collaborations

In any collaboration between two or more business entities, it is important to define at the beginning of the collaboration precisely how IP is to be handled. This pertains to IP that is brought into the collaboration as well as IP that is developed through the collaboration.

IP that is brought into the collaboration generally remains the property of the original IP owner with a license provided to the other parties to use the IP in the context of the collaboration only. It is important to document the IP that is brought into the collaboration and the specific rights that are being granted to the other parties. The best practice is to document the fact that there are no licensing rights, implied or otherwise, to the original IP or derivative IP outside the context of the specific rights granted in the collaboration.

Regarding IP that is developed during collaboration between two or more parties, the best practice is generally to agree up front that ownership of different parts of the IP, or different types of IP, will be assigned to one of the collaborating parties, with specific rights granted back to the other parties in the context of the collaboration. For example, if a software company and a bank collaborate on a database for institutional banking customers, the collaboration agreement might specify that the software company owns all of the software patents and copyrights that are developed in the collaboration, since these may be useful to the software company in other markets, but that the bank is given an exclusive, worldwide license specifically within the financial markets to any patents, trademarks, copyrights, and trade secrets that arise out of the collaboration, providing the bank an important competitive advantage in its specific market.

It is almost always best to NOT assign joint ownership of collaboratively developed IP to multiple parties, although intuitively this may seem like the easiest and fairest approach. The overarching reason to not assign joint ownership of IP to different parties in a collaboration is that the parties typically have different overall strategic objectives and business models, and therefore will leverage a specific piece of IP differently. In the example of the software company and bank collaboration above, if the bank jointly owned any patents, it would be in a position to license, even for free, the collaboratively developed patents to third parties in other market segments in which the bank did not compete but where the software company did. Similarly, if the software company jointly owned any trademarks collaboratively developed, it might not be motivated to spend a lot of money building the brand value of the trademarks but could subsequently leverage those marks in other market segments, potentially impacting the brand strategy of the bank. Since either party of jointly owned IP may basically do what it likes with the IP, including license it away for free, it potentially undermines the exclusive rights of the IP and makes it useless.

35. Employment Agreements

Like collaboration agreements, employment agreements should outline, at the beginning of the engagement, specifically how IP is to be handled. It is generally best practice for a company to get agreement from the employee that they will assign the rights, and support the prosecution, of any intellectual property that they develop while working for the employer. A good practice is to have the employee list in the employment agreement any intellectual property that he or she may have developed prior to the employment and to which he or she wishes to retain rights, particularly if it is not publically documented. It can then be specified in the employment agreement that any other intellectual property developed by the employee in the area of the company's current or future potential business (generally at the company's discretion) is to be assigned to the company. Many employment agreements have carve-out provisions that allow an employee to maintain ownership of intellectual property developed by the employee on his or her own time in areas outside of the company's current or future potential business.

Many companies have IP policies in which inventors are given a financial bonus or a portion of any licensing royalties resulting from their inventions. These IP policies are usually drafted and managed separately from the employment agreement to provide flexibility in changing the policy and consistency in implementing the same policy companywide. In some countries, it is illegal to force an employee to assign IP to the employer without providing them licensing royalties. You should consult with employment attorneys to ensure compliance with local laws.

Contractor agreements in particular must very clearly specify terms regarding IP rights since the default ownership of IP in many cases lies with the original developer of the IP, even if they are being paid by someone else.

Employment agreements should also include specific terms regarding the nondisclosure of confidential information. This should include both (i) terms that restrict an employee from disclosing the company's confidential intellectual property to any third parties during their employment with the company and for a period of time thereafter, often one to three years, as well as (ii) terms that restrict the employee from disclosing to the company any confidential information that they may have obtained from third parties, since the receipt of this type of information can create a liability for the company. These nondisclosure terms are sometimes outlined in a separate nondisclosure or confidentiality agreement. Although non-compete agreements are not enforceable in all states, nondisclosure agreements are, and they can sometimes prevent an employee from effectively going to work for a competitor because of the liability that they create for the "defecting" employee and competitor should the employee disclose, even inadvertently, any of their former company's confidential information to the competitor.

Non-compete agreements are enforced in some jurisdictions (such as many Eastern US states) and not others (such as many Western US states and some foreign countries). Even in jurisdictions that enforce non-compete agreements, such agreements are restricted in scope to a reasonable time, geography, and industry. The law disfavors limitations on a person's employment. However, if a business owner sells their business and the sales agreement has non-compete terms, those terms might be enforceable even in states that reject such terms for individuals. Likewise, if a patent owner sells a patent, the new owner may exclude the previous owner's use of the claimed invention unless the seller has a grant-back clause.

36. Secure Workplace and IT

Intellectual property must pass the test of novelty or confidentiality (or both). It is therefore critical when developing and protecting intellectual property that the work environment be secure. In the case of patents, for example, any information that becomes publically known before the patent is filed is considered prior art and cannot be the basis for a patent claim. Similarly, trade secrets that become publically known immediately lose all of their value.

Stealing confidential IP or disclosing confidential information is a crime but can often be hard to prove and hard to prosecute. The best defense to IP theft is to keep IP development contained to a secure workplace and IP environment. A system that restricts and tracks access to IP will help to detect, identify, and prosecute IP theft. The stronger these protection systems are, the more aggressively courts are willing to prosecute IP theft in general.

Conclusion

This manual has addressed the fundamental of patents and how to develop them. It all starts with answering the core question: What is the invention?

This is answered by stating how the innovation solves a problem or creates a benefit, and by defining what is novel and non-obvious about the innovation. All of the detailed invention description and prosecution needs to be built upon the foundation of the core invention.

Patent strategy and patent valuation, not addressed in this manual, are important, additional considerations when determining why pursuing a patent may make sense. The value of a patent is highly contextual and can vary dramatically based on the use of the patent, the entity that owns the patent, and the invention itself. Before spending the time and money to protect an invention, it is important to start by considering the overall business objectives and how the patent will be used to further those objectives. The decision to protect and invention through a patent needs to be made within the overall intellectual property strategy and the overall strategy of the business. Once the value of a patent to the business is well defined, this manual should provide an excellent reference for crafting robust and highly defensible patents.

Welcome to the world of protecting inventions!

APPENDIX A

Sample Invention Disclosure

XYZ Company Docket # _____

Related XYZ Dockets _____

Related Patent Applications _____

Related Patents _____

Disposition of ID:

Trade Secret ____; Provisional Patent Application (PPA)____; Utility Patent Application _____; Design Patent Application ____; and/or Foreign Filing (PCT) _____.

Patent maintenance fee due dates _____

Licensed:

    a.   Licensee: _____

    b.   Date: _____

    c.   Period (Duration): _____

    d.   Cross License? _____

    e.   Royalty:

        i.   Amount? _____

      ii.   Dates due? _____

Inventor Information

1. Name of invention: _____

2. Inventor(s) name, address, telephone, and e-mail (list all who have contributed to the invention other than in a technical assistance sense, i.e., coding, mechanical rendition, models, mock-ups, prototypes, technical support, etc.):

3. Description of the invention (attach) includes:

    a.   Purpose

    b.   Drawings, including annotated flowcharts

    c.   Code may be used to explain software-implemented inventions when the code is the best way to describe the invention but not as a substitute for describing the software function—code usually augments the description of software and system architecture but does not replace it

    d.   Algorithms and dimensions may be described in math format, however, algorithms should also have a logic flowchart

    e.   A written description of parts, components, or elements in reference to the drawings or flowcharts (please number each drawing sequentially and each element on a drawing using the drawing number as prefix, for example elements in Figure 1 are numbered sequentially 100, 102, 104 et. seq. and in Figure 2, 200, 202, and 204 et. seq.—use the same element number throughout the specification)

    f.   Use of invention (implementation)

    g.   Advantages of invention over existing technology

4. Circumstances and date of conception (conception is when the invention can be understood by a "person of ordinary skill in the art" (POSITA) who may reduce the invention to practice without undue experimentation—and the invention is ready for patenting by preparing a patent application understood by a POSITA):

    a.   When did you think of the invention?

    b.   How did you think of the invention (experimentation, problem solving, unexpected results, collaboration, etc.)?

5. Reduction to practice:

    a.   Has the invention been built in whole or part?

    b.   If so, when?

    c.   Where can the invention (or a record of it) be found?

6. Public disclosure:

    a.   Has the invention been made public by anyone in any way?

    b.   If yes: by who, when, and under what circumstances?

    c.   If the invention was made public by a person other than an inventor, did the party disclosing the invention have knowledge of the invention from an inventor or an XYZ employee or contractor?

    d.   If yes, describe the circumstance and when the disclosure occurred.

    e.   If it has been published, in what publication did it appear and when?

    f.   Has the invention been described in an article submitted for publication?

      i.   If yes, to which media outlet and when will it be published?

      ii.   Is it subject to peer review prior to publication?

      iii.   If yes, by who and when?

g.   Is a description of the invention publicly available in any way? If yes, explain.

h.   Have printed or electronic materials describing the inventions, a sample or demo been sent to a customer? If so, when?

i.   What is the product release date?

7.   Sales:

a.   Has the invention been offered for sale (must be ready for patenting)? If yes, when and to whom?

b.   Has the invention been sold (must be ready for patenting)? If yes, when and to whom?

8.   Alternatives (other ways to build or perform your invention)?

9.   Alternative uses (Other uses for the invention)?

10.   Is there a component, piece of equipment, computer code, specific material, etc. that is critical to your invention? If yes, what is it? Describe in detail.

11.   State of the art: (DO NOT USE THE TERM *PRIOR ART*)

a.   What technology is in existence prior to the invention that that is closest to the invention and its use?

b.   Is there something that performs the same function as the invention but in a different way?

c.   Do you know of patents or patent applications on similar technology? If yes, identify it by number, inventor name, and title only, but do not describe or discuss the technology.

12. Art search:

    a. If your invention did not exist, how would you solve the problem that it solved and where would you find the solution, i.e., to whom or where would you look for a solution (not yourself)?

    b. Where, other than patents, would you search to find your invention or one similar to it—publications, technical journals, etc.?

13. Prior filings (invention disclosure, provisional patent application, utility patent application, or design patent application):

    a. Type of filing: _____

    b. Date of filing: _____

    c. Serial (docket) number: _____

    d. Where filed (country)? _____

14. Where and when did you conceive your invention described in this document?

15. Were you employed by or rendering services to XYZ when you conceived or reduced this invention to practice?

16. Were you employed by or rendering services to an entity other than XYZ when you conceived or reduced this invention to practice? If yes, to whom?

17. Do you have an agreement with XYZ to assign this invention to it?

18. Do you have an agreement to assign this invention to an entity other than XYZ? (Please attach a copy of this agreement if not confidential.)

19. Do you claim ownership of the invention disclosed in this document?

20. Did you use XYZ facilities, equipment, personnel, IT, or resources in the creation, development, or conception of this invention?

21. Was any equipment or facilities used in the development of the invention which was funded by or belongs to any government agency? If yes, please describe in detail.

22. Identify your supervisor and coworkers who have knowledge of this invention:

23. Did you keep a record of this invention?

24. If there is record of this invention, other than this document, where is it recorded or stored?

25. Have you disclosed this invention to anyone? If yes who, when, where, and under what circumstances? Was the disclosure subject to a confidentiality agreement? If there was a confidentiality agreement, please provide a copy to the Legal department.

26. Have you visited any vendor or technology partner in the same technology field as this invention and in the course of the visit signed a visitor's log? If yes:

    a. Identify the entity and person visited and date of visit.

    b. Did the log or attached document require that you keep information disclosed to you during the visit confidential? If yes, do you have a copy of what you signed? If yes, provide a copy to the Legal department.

    c. When signing a visitor's log, did you assign intellectual property rights that pertain to the technology to which you were exposed while visiting the host? If yes, did the host's technology pertain to this field of invention? If yes, please describe the technology.

    d. Was this invention conceived during or part of a joint development project with another entity, i.e., a partner, vendor, or client of XYZ? If yes, describe the project in detail, including the place (premises) and date of the invention, and identify the parties that have knowledge of the invention disclosed above.

27. Additional notes or comments:

I am the inventor of the above-described invention.

Signed: _____

Print Name: _____

Date: _____

Read, witnessed, and understood: _____

Print Name: _____

Date: _____

Read, witnessed, and understood: _____

Print Name: _____

Date: _____

APPENDIX B

Requirements for Inventorship

AN INVENTOR MUST CONTRIBUTE TO THE CONCEPTION OF THE INVENTION

The definition for inventorship can be simply stated: "The threshold question in determining inventorship is who conceived the invention. Unless a person contributes to the conception of the invention, he is not an inventor. ... Insofar as defining an inventor is concerned, reduction to practice, *per se*, is irrelevant [except for simultaneous conception and reduction to practice, *Fiers v. Revel*, 984 F.2d 1164, 1168, 25 USPQ2d 1601, 1604-05 (Fed. Cir. 1993)]. One must contribute to the conception to be an inventor." *In re Hardee*, 223 USPQ 1122, 1123 (Comm'r Pat. 1984). See also *Board of*

Education ex rel. Board of Trustees of Florida State Univ. v. American Bioscience Inc., 333 F.3d 1330, 1340, 67 USPQ2d 1252, 1259 (Fed. Cir. 2003) ("Invention requires conception." With regard to the inventorship of chemical compounds, an inventor must have a conception of the specific compounds being claimed. "[G]eneral knowledge regarding the anticipated biological properties of groups of complex chemical compounds is insufficient to confer inventorship status with respect to specifically claimed compounds."); *Ex parte Smernoff,* 215 USPQ 545, 547 (Bd. App. 1982) ("one who suggests an idea of a result to be accomplished, rather than the means of accomplishing it, is not an co-inventor"). See MPEP § 2138.04 – § 2138.05 for a discussion of what evidence is required to establish conception or reduction to practice.[70]

REQUIREMENTS FOR JOINT INVENTORSHIP

The inventive entity for a particular application is based on some inventive contribution to at least one of the claims by each of the named inventors. "Inventors may apply for a patent jointly even though (1) they did not physically work together or at the same time, (2) each did not make the same type or amount of contribution, or (3) each did not make a contribution to the subject matter of every claim of the patent." 35 USC 116. "[T]he statute neither states nor implies that two inventors can be 'joint inventors' if they have had no

---

[70]http://www.uspto.gov/web/offices/pac/mpep/s2137.html

contact whatsoever and are completely unaware of each other's work." What is required is some "quantum of collaboration or connection." In other words, "[f]or persons to be joint inventors under Section 116, there must be some element of joint behavior, such as collaboration or working under common direction, one inventor seeing a relevant report and building upon it or hearing another's suggestion at a meeting." *Kimberly-Clark Corp. v. Procter & Gamble Distrib. Co.,* 973 F.2d 911, 916-17, 23 USPQ2d 1921, 1925-26 (Fed. Cir. 1992); *Moler v. Purdy,* 131 USPQ 276, 279 (Bd. Pat. Inter. 1960) ("it is not necessary that the inventive concept come to both [joint inventors] at the same time").

Each joint inventor must generally contribute to the conception of the invention. A co-inventor need not make a contribution to every claim of a patent. A contribution to one claim is enough. "The contributor of any disclosed means of a means-plus-function claim element is a joint inventor as to that claim, unless one asserting sole inventorship can show that the contribution of that means was simply a reduction to practice of the sole inventor's broader concept." *Ethicon Inc. v. United States Surgical Corp.,* 135 F.3d 1456, 1460-63, 45 USPQ2d 1545, 1548-1551 (Fed. Cir. 1998). (The electronics technician who contributed to one of the two alternative structures in the specification to define "the means for detaining" in a claim limitation was held to be a joint inventor.)[71]

---

[71] http://www.uspto.gov/web/offices/pac/mpep/s2137.html

THE INVENTOR IS NOT REQUIRED TO REDUCE THE INVENTION TO PRACTICE

Difficulties arise in separating members of a team effort, where each member of the team has contributed something, into those members that actually contributed to the conception of the invention (such as the physical structure or operative steps) and those members that merely acted under the direction and supervision of the conceivers. *Fritsch v. Lin*, 21 USPQ2d 1737, 1739 (Bd. Pat. App. & Inter. 1991) (The inventor "took no part in developing the procedures...for expressing the EPO gene in mammalian host cells and isolating the resulting EPO product." However, "it is not essential for the inventor to be personally involved in carrying out process steps...where implementation of those steps does not require the exercise of inventive skill."); *In re DeBaun*, 687 F.2d 459, 463, 214 USPQ 933, 936 (CCPA 1982) ("there is no requirement that the inventor be the one to reduce the invention to practice so long as the reduction to practice was done on his behalf").

See also *Mattor v. Coolegem*, 530 F.2d 1391, 1395, 189 USPQ 201, 204 (CCPA 1976) (one following oral instructions is viewed as merely a technician); *Tucker v. Naito*, 188 USPQ 260, 263 (Bd. Pat. Inter. 1975) (inventors need not "personally construct and test their invention"); and *Davis v. Carrier*, 81 F.2d 250, 252, 28 USPQ 227, 229 (CCPA 1936) (non-inventor's work was merely that of a skilled mechanic carrying out the details of a plan devised by another).[72]

---

[72] http://www.uspto.gov/web/offices/pac/mpep/s2137.html

APPENDIX C

Duty of Disclosure
Federal Regulations

37 C.F.R. 1.56 Duty to disclose information material to patentability.

(a) A patent by its very nature is affected with a public interest. The public interest is best served, and the most effective patent examination occurs when, at the time an application is being examined, the Office is aware of and evaluates the teachings of all **information material to patentability**. Each individual associated with the filing and prosecution of a patent application has a duty of candor and good faith in dealing with the Office, which includes a duty to disclose to the Office all information known to that individual to be material to patentability as defined in this section. The duty to disclose information exists with respect to each pending claim until the claim is cancelled or withdrawn from consideration, or the application becomes abandoned. Information material to the patentability of a claim that is cancelled or withdrawn from consideration need not be submitted if the information is not material to the patentability of any claim remaining under consideration in the application. There is no duty to submit information that is not material to the patentability of any existing claim. The duty to disclose all information known to be material to patentability is deemed to be satisfied if all information known to be material to patentability of any claim issued in a patent was cited by the Office or submitted to the Office in the manner prescribed by § 1.97(b)-(d) and 1.98. However, no patent will be granted on an application in connection with which fraud on the Office was practiced or attempted or the duty of disclosure was violated through bad faith or intentional misconduct. The Office encourages applicants to carefully examine:

1. Prior art cited in search reports of a foreign patent office in a counterpart application, and

2. The closest information over which individuals associated with the filing or prosecution of a patent application believe any pending claim patentably defines, to make sure that any material information contained therein is disclosed to the Office.

(b) Under this section, information is material to patentability when it is not cumulative to information already of record or being made of record in the application, and

1. It establishes, by itself or in combination with other information, a *prima facie* case of unpatentability of a claim; or

2. It refutes, or is inconsistent with, a position the applicant takes in:

    a. Opposing an argument of unpatentability relied on by the Office, or

    b. Asserting an argument of patentability.

A *prima facie* case of unpatentability is established when the information compels a conclusion that a claim is unpatentable under the preponderance of evidence, burden-of-proof standard, giving each term in the claim its broadest reasonable construction consistent with the specification, and before any consideration is given to evidence which may be submitted in an attempt to establish a contrary conclusion of patentability.

(c) Individuals associated with the filing or prosecution of a patent application within the meaning of this section are:

(1) Each inventor named in the application;

(2) Each attorney or agent who prepares or prosecutes the application; and

(3) Every other person who is substantively involved in the preparation or prosecution of the application and who is associated with the inventor, with the assignee or with anyone to whom there is an obligation to assign the application.

(d) Individuals other than the attorney, agent, or inventor may comply with this section by disclosing information to the attorney, agent, or inventor.

(e) In any continuation-in-part application, the duty under this section includes the duty to disclose to the Office all information known to the person to be material to patentability, as defined in paragraph (b) of this section, which became available between the filing date of the prior application and the national or PCT international filing date of the continuation-in-part application.

Dirk Brown is the Director of the Faber Entrepreneurship Center and a Faculty Member at both the Darla Moore School of Business and the College of Engineering and Computing at the University of South Carolina. Dr. Brown is a seasoned executive with a strong track record of developing, marketing, and licensing disruptive, proprietary technologies. He is the CEO of Pandoodle Corporation, an international media technology company, and has previously held senior executive positions in several technology companies. He holds over 25 patents, has written over 30 technical papers and journal articles, and is an active member in a number of professional societies.

Dale Hogue combines his experience in business and law to monetize intellectual property by IP licensing and M&A as a member of Grey Gold Advisors, LLC. He has litigated intellectual property rights, provided strategic IP planning, counseled clients, conducted product clearance, infringement and validity opinions, drafted and negotiated licensing agreements, and practiced before the United States Patent and Trademark Office. He is an experienced licensing executive having sold and licensed patents and other intellectual property. Mr. Hogue was in the investment banking business and served on the investment committee of an IP holding company, formed joint ventures and assisted startups in their formation and capitalization.